Shawn & Gabrielle

All the best

Kurt

The
Golden

Flame

The Heart and Soul of
Remarkable Leadership

Dr. Keith Merron

Published, printed and distributed in the United States.

Published by:
Avista Press
1083 Vine Street
Suite 515
Healdsburg, California 95448
415-488-4003

Library of Congress Control Number:
LCCN: 2009914218

Publisher's Cataloging-in-Publication Data

Merron, Keith, 1956-
The golden flame: the heart and soul of remarkable leadership / by Dr. Keith Merron.
p. cm.

ISBN: 978-0-615-34221-4

1. Leadership. 2. Management.   I. Title.
HD57.7 M476 2010
658.4`092 —dc22

First printing January 2010

Cover design by Detta Penna

Interior design by Illumination Graphics
www.illuminationgraphics.com

January 15, 2010

Dear Reader,

This copy of *The Golden Flame: Searching for the Heart and Soul of Remarkable Leadership* is offered to you in the spirit of sharing what I believe to be some profound and time-tested ways of understanding leadership that for too long have been bypassed or not well-expressed amidst the deluge of leadership books offered in the market. Its contents and form are all designed to cause you to think deeply and perhaps differently than ever before about the nature of great leadership and more importantly, the nature of leadership inside yourself. I share this book in hopes that it captures your imagination and ignites the golden flame inside you.

If you would like to learn more about my work and me please take a look at my website as well: www.remarkableleaders.com. Feel free to also reach out to me through email if you want to correspond directly.

I wish you good reading and hope that this book serves your unfolding journey as a leader.

Warm Wishes,

Keith Merron
kmerron3@comcast.net

Dedication

———— ✦ ————

This book is dedicated to my children, Josh and Maya,
who inspire me to become the best father I can be
and who teach me so much about love, patience,
and a sense of wonder.

Testimonials for the Golden Flame

"This is a book I have enjoyed watching develop and I strongly recommend reading it. Combining as it does the unique insights of a distinguished group of remarkable leaders with the observational perspective on life philosophy of Dr. Merron, it will provide a valuable roadmap to those seeking guidance and wisdom as a leader."

> David Crane
> President and CEO
> NewHope Bariatrics, Inc.
> Former CEO of MedCath, Inc.

"Finally, here is a book on leadership that doesn't follow the rather worn five-step approach to leadership. Keith Merron's thoughtful research has uncovered some critical leadership truths that will inspire each reader to discover not only the key to being a remarkable leader but, more importantly, how to find the purpose that will drive their success. This is a must read for anyone who is serious about finding the golden flame that burns inside each of us. It will also be a must read for everyone on my executive team."

> James R. Pouliot
> CEO
> California State Automobile Association

"This book is Keith's very personal journey to discovering what makes good leaders. Rather than provide pat answers, the book encourages us to ask deeper questions and go on our own personal journey, which is where meaningful learning and discovery take place. The book's case studies illustrate that while there may be consistent characteristics good leaders exhibit – as documented by many other books – these are really just symptoms of something more fundamentally important. Keith challenges us to examine our own purpose and expectations, and their sources – in that way, this is a helpful guide to choosing, developing and becoming better leaders."

> Eric Fish
> Former CEO of Golden Gate Software

"As someone who works with hundreds of CEOs, I thoroughly recommend "The Golden Flame." Keith Merron has captured the soul of those rare individuals that he refers to as "Remarkable Leaders." Using powerful and compelling stories, Keith has shattered the popular stereotype of the charismatic leader. He found that the essence of the most effective leaders has nothing to do with their personalities or "management styles." The characteristics that define remarkable leaders are their clarity of purpose, rock-solid values and quiet confidence."

Paul Witkay
Founder & CEO
Alliance of Chief Executives

In one word, your draft of The Golden Flame is terrific! I loved the premise, the tone and the content. I started reading it because I made a commitment to you to review it. I finished the draft chapters because they completely captured my interest.

– Your approach to leadership is unique and realistically addresses the critically important issue of how individuals can access their own leadership potential

– I was touched, sometimes deeply, by your portrayal of the leaders you met with and their stories. You did a wonderful job of capturing the essence of Chauncey.

– The messages in the book ring true to me and are consistent with the behaviors and belief systems of the handful of outstanding leaders I have been fortunate enough to know.

– The book's message is also consistent with the way my view of leadership has evolved throughout the years. Thirty years ago, I thought that leadership was defined by the attributes you see in people like JFK - quick, articulate, visionary, attractive, etc. And, with that as my template, I never, ever expected to become a leader. Over the years, I have come to learn what your book is proposing; namely, that trusting my own inner voice and being fully committed to the directions it points to is the wellspring of my personal leadership.

Ric Rudman
Former COO of Electrical Power Research Institute

"Thank you for the opportunity to read your book. I have to say that I didn't expect to find my struggle within my own mind right there on your pages, but I certainly did! The internal questions, self-doubt, and immense desire to have a sense of purpose – and thus conviction and direction - read like my own personal story. So, I know you speak the truth. Leadership and confidence and presence does come from inside. It does come from having a bigger game than yourself at stake. Your book was a great reminder of that for me. THANKS!"

Cate Sabbitini
Former EVP of Sales & Marketing at Iconix
Biosciences and VP of Customer Relations at Incyte

"Keith Merron's The Golden Flame provides insightful observations on the essence of strong leadership and helpful discussion on how to capture your own authentic leadership potential. I recommend this book to anyone who is, or will be, in a leadership position, from PTA chairperson to Fortune 500 CEO. Read, learn, enjoy."

Bannus Hudson
Former CEO of Lenscrafters and BevMo

"Thank you for sending your book. I thoroughly enjoyed reading it. I found it extremely insightful. I especially appreciated the humility, transparency, and vulnerability of your writing style as you shared your own struggles searching for the Golden Flame in your life. As you know it has been my great privilege to be the leader of numerous organizations, some of much size and scope. Your observations resonated with my spirit as I have strived to follow my own inner compass and be a more profound leader. There is much wisdom in your book— candidly, it's the best I've read on the subject of leadership. I know it will be a blessing to many people.

Keep up the great work. It will make a difference in many lives."

Bill Williams
Former President of Pyxis, Inc.

"Each of us sets our sights on our apex, our top jobs and our vision for our future as leaders – and its how we get there that defines our true leadership. It's so easy to get caught in the trappings of leadership: power, charisma, ambition, and force. We watch and learn from others, we use our compass, and set our engines full speed ahead. Then life happens! The Golden Flame *is an incredibly powerful book written about leaders who have stepped into a new framework of leadership – one we can all learn from.* The Golden Flame *helps us see through the fog of power, into a clear light of soulful, purposeful, values-driven leadership. Life is not predictable. Great leaders must learn to weather the storms. Most importantly, great leaders need to learn to acknowledge that the light comes from within, and burns inside of each of us – each person has a Golden Flame that when ignited, will become a leadership beacon for a lifetime!"*

Judith E. Glaser
Best Selling Author (Creating WE; DNA of Leadership; 42 Rules for Creating WE); CEO of Benchmark Communications, Inc. and Founder of Creating WE Institute

"The Golden Flame" is Keith Merron's take on a kind of leadership so authentic that it can't be laughed off. He is one of the most remarkable business writers out there today. Intense, intelligent, and sincere."

Mike Finley, co-author, *The New Why Teams Don't Work*

"Keith's book brings together an impressive array of perspectives — from business research to the power of psychological archetypes — to get at the alchemy of leadership. Neither a cookie cutter formula nor an innate capacity, leadership is a journey involving deep self-understanding and commitment. Keith's writing coveys the subtleties of leadership in simple and compelling stories, both his own and those of the many leaders whose experiences are documented in the book. All in all, its a fun read and a great resource for those interested in walking the path of leadership."

Paul Downs
Strategic Planning and Organization Development Consultant

"The Golden Flame is a must read for anyone interested in improving their own relationship to power and leadership. Keith's very open inner journey and relationship to his own leadership is powerful and a stark contrast to books focused on ego-led outer manifestations of leadership. By sharing his own experience of face to face interviews of remarkable leaders, this book is not a "how to" but a "wow" – opening a door to completely new ways of leading authentically and in service to something larger than ourselves. I continue to benefit by applying the principles into my work with my own company, clients and community. Highly recommended.

Steve Tennant
Managing Director, Tennant Consulting

Keith Merron's "The Golden Flame" tackles the subject of how to lead from a personal perspective. His portrayal of leadership provides a soulful journey that takes the reader to the core of where great leadership comes from. Rich profiles of leaders demonstrate the essential leadership foundations of self-knowledge and purpose. The book weaves together compelling descriptions of corporate and community leaders who demonstrate passion and purpose in their leadership with a model of self-understanding grounded in the theoretical perspectives of experts. Keith Merron inserts his personal perspectives and leadership struggles, bringing the concepts to life.

Jeanie Fay-Snow
Executive Coach

TABLE OF CONTENTS

————— ✧ —————

INTRODUCTION

⸻ ◇ ⸻

This book is not about ordinary leadership or about those who've met the criteria of traditional leadership success. It's about leaders whose greatness has been achieved by making decisions based on a deep desire to serve. It's about people in positions of authority who do not abuse that authority but instead make a positive difference in the people they meet—who touch others by their presence. It's about people acting not out of ego but from an inner source of wisdom. It's about people who lift us up and make us proud to be a part of their effort, who can show us not just who we are but what we might become. And, perhaps most importantly, it is a clarion call to find one's own leadership core and to stop seeking it in others. In short, it's about what I call the golden flame.

A golden flame is a fire that burns within. And not just any fire, for many of us burn hot—in anger, or personal ambition, or greed, or resentment. A golden flame is different. It's a fire of passion directed toward a cause greater than oneself, ignited by determination, caring, and a relentless commitment to live a life of generosity—to make things better. It is a fire that burns golden from integrity and stays lit from the inner solidity of the person who contains it; when its heat touches others, they are uplifted, for it ignites the flame in themselves.

Too often, the charisma of self-serving leaders does the opposite. Their desire for acclaim casts a shadow over the needs of others. The leadership history of Michael Eisner, for example, defines the archetype of a leader with an all-too-typical Achilles heel. For many years Eisner could do no wrong. He was CEO at The Walt Disney Company, for decades one of the most admired companies in the world. When Eisner arrived in the early 1980s, however, the Disney juggernaut had stalled. Its reputation as the leader in movie-length animation had eroded from a steady loss of top talent and the absence of Walt Disney at the helm. While the brand remained solid, the business reality lagged far behind. Under Eisner's welcome leadership the company grew by leaps and bounds, fueled to a large extent by decisions that Eisner spearheaded, such as reinvigorating Disney's flagship animation division.

Wall Street loved Eisner. He was brash, charismatic, and confident. Every year he was listed among the top CEOs for performance, earnings, and clout. To the trained eye, however, there were signs that all was not well. On his way to the top, Eisner had alienated many of the members of his executive team, including Jeffrey Katzenberg, who led the then-thriving animation division, and Roy Disney, Walt Disney's nephew and a spiritual reminder of the company's storied past. As chronicled in the thoroughly researched *Disney War* by James B. Stewart, this disaffection, along with declining box office success, ill-considered theme park developments, and a costly Internet investment that went awry, ultimately sounded Eisner's death knell in 2004 when he left Disney after a no-confidence vote of the board.

Few foresaw this downfall. Most were enamored with Eisner's magnetic personality and with the results he obtained, which were extraordinary—at least for a while. But to those who looked closely, Eisner's fall was inevitable, and brings to mind the story of Icarus, son of the Greek craftsman Daedalus, both of whom were imprisoned by King Minos of Crete. To escape their captivity, Daedalus created two pairs of wings using feathers, wood, and wax. He cautioned Icarus not to fly too close to the sun, but Icarus, intoxicated by his ability to fly, soared too high, the wax melted, and he fell to his death.

In our modern and telegenic society, we are seduced by personality and by people who can talk a good game. They entice us with their promises, and for a while we get lost in their dream. This was Eisner's appeal. But when such dreams are coupled with a need for recognition and power, they can quickly turn into nightmares. Corporate graveyards are filled with people who convinced an organization to believe in their greatness, only to find out that they could not back up the dream, or worse, that the dream was a con.

Eisner's rise was based not on clear vision, great execution, an integrated strategy, or strong personal character but on the tendency of people to surrender to a vision without paying much attention to the details. Stewart's account of Eisner, and the accounts of so many others who have written on the subject, strongly suggest that it was Eisner's deep need to control others, his tendency to micro-manage, and his pattern over time of stripping the soul from a brand in order to maximize short-term results that ultimately led to his final demise. And sadly, this is not an unusual scenario. Numerous ill-fated acquisitions have gone sour because they did not follow any strategy other than "bigger is better," often driven by a leader's need for power or headlines rather than long-term fiduciary interest. That's short-sighted leadership and we all too often fall prey to its seduction.

In contrast, each of the leaders mentioned in this book has a golden flame within them, one that ignites the flames of others. It's the mark of an extraordinary leader. Leadership that embodies a golden flame doesn't come from position or line of command, though such people do command our respect, nor from being a terrific facilitator, though people who embody the golden flame are often wonderful guides and coaches. It is something special, the kind of leadership that most of us hunger for and all too rarely experience.

> *Great leaders have a*
> *golden flame inside them,*
> *one that ignites the*
> *golden flame in others.*

The focus of this book is on the behaviors, attitudes, and ways of being that characterize these remarkable leaders and that I believe will define a new era of leadership and organizational life. And unlike most books written about leadership, this one focuses on the humanity and heart that lie within a successful leader rather than on their impressive achievements. We will learn not from superstar CEOs who we've already seen on the covers of magazines but from leaders who really lead—those who are committed more to their companies than to their own publicity files, who resonate with genuine passion and humility. And rather than emphasizing the textbook qualities that characterize great leaders, we seek the "holy grail" of leadership—to understand and elucidate the primary causes that inspire extraordinary leadership. We already know, for example, that leadership has something to do with vision, courage, determination, and emotional intelligence. The bigger and more profound question is why do some people embody these while others settle for watered-down facsimiles?

How I Approached the Subject of Leadership

Questions kept coursing through me as I began this book. What does it take to become a remarkable leader? What is the journey? Why do some people take it while others do not? And why do some who take the journey then fall from grace? Anyone's life journey, yours and mine included, has mythological dimensions. Think of Jason and the Argonauts or Huckleberry Finn, whose adventures were fraught with intrigue and peril. The same is true of the journey to leadership. No one becomes a true leader without facing monsters in the outer world and demons in their inner world.

And so to understand the forces that give rise to extraordinary leadership, I sought a more personal approach, one where I would meet with and learn from those who seem to embody the values that I was seeking, who were tangibly connected to their heart and soul. By heart and soul I mean the essence of their identity, the core of qualities that makes them tick, that fuels their passion and commitment. I was interested in their spirit, and how that spirit inspired others (*spirit* and *inspire* come from the same root—the word for "breathe"). In short, I was interested in their journey of becoming.

My search for remarkable leaders began with a set of criteria, and the bar was necessarily high.

1. They must be a current or former COO, President, Managing Partner, Executive Director, or CEO with significant responsibility for developing the strategy and culture of their organization.

2. Their organization must be doing something unique or distinct within their industry.

3. They must have distinguished themselves in some way. They must be path creators, not pathfinders or path followers.

4. Their leadership must be inspiring, empowering, or both.

I then reached out to about 200 professional acquaintances— colleagues, clients, and interested friends—and asked them: *Who have you personally worked with who meets the criteria I have described?* Even though my network included prominent executives throughout the country, most people replied: "Sorry, none come to mind."

How could this be? Was it because there aren't a lot of great leaders in the work world today? Thousands of men and women occupy leadership positions, but that doesn't make them great, or even good, leaders. The world is full of people in leadership positions who are there for un-leaderly reasons: They went to the right school, they are well connected, they are highly ambitious, and/or they hung around long enough for seniority to triumph over competence (remember the "Peter Principle"?). These features of a person's life may be helpful to having a successful career, but they have nothing to do with great leadership.

Thankfully, I didn't strike out entirely. Enough recommendations were made to give me a place to begin. Over time the list grew as the people I interviewed would say to me, "Oh, you've got to meet so and so. He/she is an extraordinary leader."

I ended up with 36 interviews, and each one had a similar feel. While the personalities of these leaders were as different as can be, they had something in common that was unmistakable, a kind of personal power that became the central theme of my experience of them. I imagined that power as a golden flame. It burned brightly in each of the people I met. It was palpable. You could feel it in their presence, see it in their eyes, and sense it in the way they carried themselves. It was not so much what they said but how they said it. And with only the occasional momentary exception, there was no tendency to seduce or charm, as one often finds in leaders enamored with their own self-reflection. I'm reminded of BALCO founder Victor Conti, who seduced hundreds of athletes, including Barry Bonds, high profile baseball player, with slick salesmanship and the lure of steroids. Many books that exalt the power of positive thinking are also guilty of advocating such manipulative come-ons. No, the leaders I found were grounded and well contained, and for this they had enormous credibility.

I spent numerous hours with each of these leaders and asked many personal questions: *How do you characterize your style of leadership? What do you care about most? What forces and events shaped who you are and how you express yourself as a leader?* Fueled by curiosity and open to surprise, I wanted to know their deeper truths rather than canned thoughts designed to impress. We explored the nature of leadership and the inner guidance that gives rise to outer effectiveness. We also talked about life, about who influenced them as a child and the people they most admired, about their hopes, dreams, and regrets, their biggest successes, and their most dismal failures. And through it all I found that the two, life and work, cannot be separated in the hearts and minds of these remarkable leaders.

In the chapters to follow you will read about Scott Johnson, whose belief that most medical research doesn't understand disease from a systemic perspective is revolutionizing the study of multiple sclerosis. You will meet Chauncey Starr, a 93-year-old wonder who continues to work full time, fueled by a deep desire to serve all of humankind. You will come to know Mimi Silbert, whose passion and commitment to people in trouble gave birth to one of the most extraordinary social institutions of our time. You will meet Robert Bobb, the city manager of Washington, D.C., who spoke about his hard life growing up on a farm and the inspiration he got from his grandmother. Although she had only a fifth-grade education, she impressed him with her abiding thirst for knowledge and for life. You will be inspired by Mary Taverna whose passion for nursing took an unexpected turn 40 years ago, causing her to be instrumental in bringing the concept of Hospice to the United States. And you will learn about Gordon Gund, who has created a business empire based on simple principles of caring and trust. Gund is also blind, and does not feel his affliction is an obstacle. Quite the opposite; he considers it a great source of learning.

Each of these leaders is powerful, although few are marquee names. Most aren't interested in notoriety, and they prefer it that way. Indeed, few of the people nominated were leaders of large companies. This caused me to wonder if great leadership and large organizations don't automatically go hand in hand, particularly when you consider the compromises that many Fortune 500 leaders must make to meet the short-term demands of Wall Street, which measures success in quarterly increments and cares more about reliable results than the cultures from which such results are created. Some people who run large companies get there not because they are great leaders but because they are skilled at playing the power games unique to these environments. Though winning such games is undeniably a valuable skill, it is not the same as true leadership, and this is what we need in a time where change is constant, predicting the future is becoming less reliable, and traditional models of management are outliving their usefulness.

How This Book Is Organized

This book is organized into three sections. The first one sets the table by exploring the notion of remarkable leadership and the challenges to achieving it. Leaders I met show that the core of greatness does not reside in behaviors, personality, or even the characteristics that typically describe great leaders such as vision, courage, and fierce resolve. Instead, it is found in three essential qualities that live deep within the soul: a clear inner compass, a powerful anchor of values, and a rock-solid sense of self.

The next section, Chapters 3 through 8, illustrates each of these three qualities in specific ways. Through the voices of the leaders I interviewed and the stories they share about their journey into leadership, you will learn about the choices and experiences that made these leaders great, which can be the source of your own greatness.

The final section inserts these essential qualities into the alchemical process of becoming a great leader while drawing on additional insights from theories of management and personality development. Are leaders born or made? What is soulful leadership? By exploring these questions, I offer guidance on how you can find the extraordinary and unique leader within you.

The Ultimate Aim of the Book

To call my journey "research" would not satisfy those who want carefully defined protocols, clear cause and effects, and the identification of specific variables to show empirically what is or isn't true. Although there has been considerable structure in my exploration, it would hardly stand up to the scrutiny of a doctoral dissertation committee. Nor does it need to, for while I started with the question of what causes great leaders to become that way, a far deeper question emerged: What is the essence of my own leadership? As a result, the research and writing of this book is more to me than an exploration of what it takes to be a great leader. It has become an odyssey—a journey toward the leadership potential inside myself. While I cannot claim to have arrived, the journey has been both exhilarating and painful, and I've learned much more than I ever expected or could even begin to measure.

Throughout the book, then, I will share some of my own thoughts and reactions to the leaders I met. In addition, I will share some of my own struggles to become a better leader, not to call attention to myself but to suggest that the journey of leadership is a very human endeavor. To the extent that my process of discovery can be revealed and shared as one person's path, perhaps you will find resonance in some of the questions I asked myself and maybe even identify with some of my answers.

Ultimately, my greatest desire is that by reading this book, you will be inspired to bring forward more of the leadership greatness inside you. But first a caveat: Becoming a great leader doesn't occur just by reading a book. If it did, we'd be surrounded by great leaders. No, learning about leadership is not the same as *becoming* a great leader. The inner qualities of great leaders are hard-won, developed over a lifetime of inquiry, dedication, commitment to self-honesty, love for human beings, and the desire to cultivate and nourish what is the best in the human race. In the 30 years that I've been studying leadership and seeking to cultivate my own, I have come to realize that *deep learning* is always an internal process. The motivation to become a better leader can only come from within. The goal is not to copy another person's path but to appreciate that each great leader you'll read about here found their leadership signature through self-examination and embracing fully who they are. This is the ultimate challenge of becoming a great leader as well as living a fulfilling life—to be yourself. It is in honor of this challenge that we begin the journey to find the Golden Flame.

CHAPTER 1

—◇—

THE PROBLEM WITH LEADERSHIP

Then there are [those]...who are endlessly
driven to seek the elusive Grail of material
success because they have lost their inner
spirit and can only look outward for identity
and meaning.

—Jean Houston

A s you walk into Delancey Street Restaurant, all seems normal—
just another appealing restaurant, one of hundreds that populate
San Francisco. Noted for its attractive location overlooking the
bay and for its tasty Mediterranean cuisine, you would likely file it away
as one of the many places to get a wonderful meal in the Bay Area—unless
you knew its history.

The restaurant is part of the Delancey Street Foundation, a nonprofit
organization dedicated to helping people who have faced difficult times
to get their life back together. Every staff member of the restaurant lives
next door at a residence home for former drug addicts, drug dealers, gang
members, murderers, and assorted multiple felons. The profits from the
restaurant, as well as from a moving company, a limousine service, and
several other businesses that operate under the Delancey Street umbrella,
go toward paying for the home.

This breakthrough concept, developed by founder Mimi Silbert, supports residents in learning a trade, reviving their self-esteem, and in getting their lives on a path toward success. The only requirements for getting into the program are that one has to have faced a significant challenge in their life—drug abuse, alcohol addiction, prison, etc.—and made a deep and abiding commitment to getting their life back on track.

When I visited the restaurant to meet with Mimi, I didn't know what to expect. I had heard from many enthusiastic patrons about Delancey Street but had never actually been there. I arrived in late afternoon, only to learn that Mimi had been called away to attend to a family crisis. The staff was preparing for the dinner crowd and was wonderfully gracious toward me. Mimi's assistant, Dawn, apologized that I hadn't received her last-minute message that Mimi would not be available.

Seizing the moment, I took the opportunity to chat with Dawn about Delancey Street and learn about how it operates. She was engaging, bright-eyed, and cheerful. After hearing how all staff members are part of the residential home, I asked her with some hesitation, "Um, are you a resident here as well?"

She smiled. "Of course. We all are. Everyone you see here is."

In fact, Delancey Street has no actual "staff." Even Mimi lives in the community like everyone else and doesn't take a salary. Delancey Street operates on a role model concept in which all residents are "staff" to each other. "Each one teach one" is the main idea, where everyone is simultaneously a learner and a teacher, a giver and a receiver. I mentioned to Dawn how impressed I was with how she carried herself. She thanked me matter-of-factly, a quality that characterized the entire conversation.

I asked another awkward question: "Why does everyone seem so friendly and gracious?" Dawn smiled again and said, "Oh, that's easy. We all want to be like Mimi."

Mimi was more than just the boss or the paymaster at Delancey Street, as I soon discovered. She modeled the kind of person that Dawn and everyone else wanted to become—honest, open, and caring, simultaneously strong and vulnerable, and infused with a generous spirit. Mimi Silbert was the keeper of Delancey Street's golden flame, exemplifying the kind of leadership that this book is about. You'll learn more about Mimi in later chapters.

As we all know, however, such leaders are few and far between. And while every generation seems to echo the same refrain, "They don't make leaders like they used to," the available research suggests that things haven't changed much over the years. According to a study at the University of Chicago in 2004, for example, public confidence in leadership across a variety of institutions—the military, the government, business, academia—has for decades remained low: on average, only about one-third of the population express a reasonable degree of confidence in their leaders.[1] Stated another way, two-thirds of the population has been dissatisfied with their leaders across all sectors for a long time. A more recent study showed a low to moderate level of confidence in leadership in every sector studied with the exception of the medical and military sectors (see Figure 1-1.)[2] As if to emphasize the point, this very same study showed that between 2007 and 2008, confidence in leadership dropped more sharply than it ever had in the history of the study.

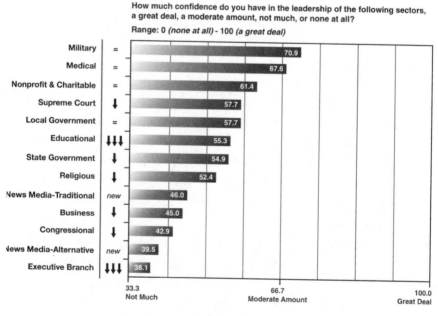

Figure 1.1

Similarly, according to the 2008-2009 Global Leadership Forecast, a bi-annual study conducted by Development Dimensions International (DDI), confidence in business leaders is at a 10-year-low. Since 1999, the level has steadily declined; in the most recent survey, only 35 percent of respondents cited a high degree of confidence in their leaders.[3]

These and other findings should come as no surprise as the media offer countless examples of leaders using their power and position for outcomes contrary to the general public's interest. What is particularly daunting, however, is the impact of such dissatisfaction on employees. In study after study, researchers have found that trust and confidence in top leadership is one of the most reliable predictors of employee satisfaction in an organization. For example, in *The Leadership Challenge*, noted leadership experts Kouzes and Posner offer that 98% of employees say they perform at a higher level when a leader who they respect encourages them.[4] Similarly, leadership style accounts for as much as 12% of variance in the level of employee commitment.[5] To the extent that there is a clear and known relationship between employee satisfaction, engagement, retention, and performance,[6] it is perplexing indeed why leaders wouldn't get the message and learn how to lead more effectively. Such findings deepen many people's concern that the holy grail of remarkable leadership will always be little more than a myth.

My own disappointment with inferior leadership began in my very first job at a once high-flying computer company that had been a pioneer in the computer industry. I had landed a position as a management trainer and quickly became initiated into the world of big-company politics. Why I had been given a position to train managers—often 10-20 years my senior—on how to manage while having no management experience myself was a mystery. Even worse, my lack of experience in the hurly-burly of corporate life, with the exception of a few short stints at a Taco Bell, Bonanza Steak House, the U. S. Department of Labor, and a local furniture delivery company, left me clueless on how to handle the politics. My boss and his boss were constantly scheming over ways to increase their clout in the company, and as an idealistic young man I was repulsed by their obsession. In seeking power and wielding it like a sword, they clearly placed their own self-interest in front of the good of the company, and on several occasions I confronted them about their ethics and choices.

After a tempestuous first year, my manager's boss took me aside and said something like, "Keith, we think you're talented, and we'd like to keep you on the team, but sometimes you're a real pain in the ass, fighting everything we put forward. So here's the deal: Either get on board or get out." Unable to reconcile their actions with my ideals, I chose the latter and he happily showed me the door.

Looking back, I wonder what I expected – that they would hang their heads in shame and say, "You're right, kid. From now on we'll really care!" I stood up to them, they made quick work of me, and I nursed that wound of disappointment for many years.

Like a lot of people, I've had spotty relationships with many of my managers and with leaders in general. One could argue that I've had unreasonable expectations, holding a standard so high that nobody could possibly meet it, or that I was searching for an idealized parent, or that the leader in me was aching to come out and that by knocking down other leaders I was somehow getting closer to ascending the throne myself—a variation of the Oedipal Myth playing out in corporate life. Perhaps there's some truth in all of that.

But in the end I'm no different from most anyone else, hungry for leaders who care about the humanness of the enterprises they run, who will remind me that this busyness we call "work" actually means something, that we are not a cog in a savage machine, and that beyond the cold face of industry there is a beating, gracious heart. It's a hunger that is rarely satisfied.

Ironically, there are as many books and articles depicting leaders as godlike figures with capacities far beyond our own as there are chronicling their dark side, showing them as tyrants, demagogues, philanderers, and worse. *Snakes in Suits*, *Bad Leadership*, *The Allure of Toxic Leaders*, and *Do as I Say, Not as I Do*—the list goes on. Such books give us a peek behind the curtain and reveal that our "gods" have feet of clay.

And so it goes, our thinking about leaders oscillating between "They are wizards" and "They are crooks." We demand an inhuman level of guidance from our leaders and then resent them for their human frailties. We build them up only to knock them down. Either way, we feel vaguely hopeless. We can neither *be* them (they're too good) nor *trust* them (they're too bad). Somehow, we have conspired to make leadership impossible – unassailable on the one hand, and "You don't want to follow them" on the other. It's a frustrating set of polarized views and equally frustrating for those who are actually trying to lead.

The dearth of strong leadership in so many organizations exacts a high price. In their book, *The Extraordinary Leader*, John Zenger and Joseph Folkman report on an extensive study that found, among many other things, that the sign of an effective leader is the prevalence of engaged employees (see Figure 1-2).[7]

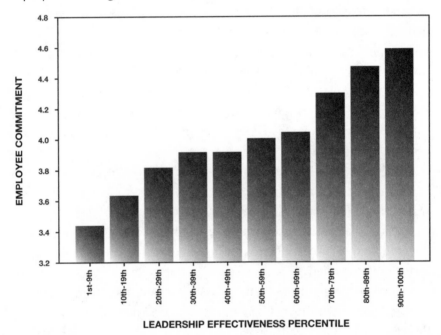

Figure 1-2: The Relationship between Leadership and Employee Commitment

In this study, they measured leadership effectiveness through both a 360-degree survey process and the strength of employee commitment to

> *We demand an inhuman level of guidance from our leaders and then resent them for their human frailties.*

a company. A clear and direct relationship emerged, as one might expect. What are particularly notable, though, are the extremes: below the 20th percentile and above the 70th percentile. This is where leadership skill matters the most. A little bit of improvement at the lower levels of leadership produces a significant improvement in employee commitment, while similar improvements at higher levels also produce a significant upswing in employee commitment. Changes in between seem to matter much less.

Also no surprise, though not commonly understood: Employee engagement directly impacts the bottom line. Consider, for example, a study by Watson Wyatt (one of the world's largest and most reputable human resources consulting firms) that surveyed over 13,000 full time U.S. workers in 2008.[8] It found that when employees are highly engaged, their companies enjoy 26 percent higher productivity, have lower turnover risk, and are more likely to attract top talent. Moreover, according to the study, highly engaged employees are twice as likely as their less engaged peers to be top performers. They also miss 20 percent fewer days of work, and three-quarters of them exceeded or far exceeded expectations in their most recent performance review. Additionally, highly engaged workers tend to be more supportive of organizational change initiatives and more resilient in the face of change. Numerous other studies including those by the Gallup Corporation show the same. In short, helping leaders or oneself to move from good to great leadership can produce a quantum leap in organizational performance.

The Hunger for Exemplary Leadership

To get a handle on what good leadership really means, we need to ask ourselves the following: *Why do we yearn for it so much? Why is it so crucial to our existence?*

A middle-level manager recently told me she was planning to leave her company. When I asked her why, she said she was disappointed in its leadership—that the gap between her expectations and what the leadership provided was too great. Among her choice words about the CEO were: "He doesn't care about the rank and file." "He isn't a good role model for the company's values." "He's unavailable." Interestingly, I know this CEO well, and my experience of this leader, shared by most of his employees, doesn't match the experience of this manager. Regardless of the truth of the CEO's effectiveness, however, it was her view that was telling, for it revealed something about the human condition.

Discussing this disappointment, it became evident to both of us that she had an idealized vision of what she wanted in a leader, and this was not the first time she had been disappointed. As she looked back over her career, she realized that she had never been satisfied with any leader. (I immediately identified with her experience.) As we poked beneath the surface of her frustration, she mentioned that she had also been disappointed with her parents, and had spent much of her adult life seeking in leaders what she didn't get from them. In her childhood memories, they just weren't there for her, playing the "Do as I say, not as I do" card far too many times. She had expected far more than she received.

It's an oft-told tale, and perhaps in some ways the hunger for great leadership reflects an unfilled need from childhood. We want to be loved, nurtured, and guided by our leaders in the same way we expected from our parents, and when our leaders don't make the grade, we get resentful and look for someone else to fill the void. Perhaps our parents did fail in the ways we often claim, but the more we blame them, the harder it is to establish our own solidity and wholeness and the healthy love of self that defines psychological well-being. And high self-esteem is at the foundation of almost all feelings of love, ease, and productive success. From Abraham Maslow's work on high-functioning human beings to Stephen Covey's work described in his book *The 7 Habits of Highly Successful People* to Martin Seligman's groundbreaking research on learned optimism and the science of happiness, the message keeps repeating itself: Self-esteem and psychological ownership of our own condition go hand in hand. So the tendency to blame leaders is often directly related to a hole that we haven't filled in ourselves.

> *The tendency to blame leaders is often directly related to a hole that we haven't filled in ourselves.*

This predisposition reminds me of how people often choose their spouses. Many noted psychologists, including Harville Hendrix, the famous couples' counselor and best-selling author, believe that we are attracted to people with strong characteristics of our parents. This represents an unconscious attempt to get from them the love that we missed while growing up. In other words, our attraction to a mate can sometimes reflect a desire to heal childhood wounds.

Of course, this doesn't mean that the desire for great leadership **always** comes from low self-esteem and an unconscious need to heal. It can also come from an innate sense that great leadership plays an important role in human organizational functioning. To the extent that we care about our organizations being run well, we care about leadership and have appropriately high standards. It is the grousing about leadership that often covers unmet needs inside oneself that can shift a natural desire for effective leadership to a game of blame and unrealistic expectation. And in Western societies, such an immature relationship to leadership is widely evident.

The anger and disappointment that many of us unleash on our leaders—"This is all your fault, not mine"—masks what I feel is the most corrosive cause of our discontent: a lack of self-esteem that no leader can ever provide. Without a strong sense of personal confidence and grounding, one is vulnerable to the seductions of phony leadership. Leaders often promise what they can never fulfill, and unsuspecting or directionless followers are all too willing to do what they're told (drink their Kool-Aid) especially if they have a pattern of idealizing their leaders. You can see this in cults and to varying degrees in many religions throughout the world.

Further complicating the picture is our modern industrial society's relationship to power—shared by many ancient cultures as well—which tends to define it as power *over* others as opposed to power *with* others. When we perceive that an authority figure is misusing their power or behaving in ways we deem as unfair, our natural reaction is to refuse their demands or push back—directly or indirectly, consciously or unconsciously. In so doing we often act petulantly, like adolescents. (This can also happen in our personal relationships.) In response, many leaders wind up treating people as children who need discipline, perpetuating a dysfunctional parent–child cycle and preventing both leaders and those they lead from breaking out of the routine. This powerful, self-reinforcing dynamic remains the dark, hidden underbelly of leadership. Both leaders and followers play a role that keeps leaders in positions of dominance and followers as submissive dependents who are never allowed to mature.

In part, this dynamic is further enabled by a belief that leaders should be all knowing and capable of extraordinary things, and too many of them fall into this trap, claiming gifts of insight and infallible competencies while masking their natural shortcomings. This tendency mirrors the follower's desire that such claims be true, reflecting both a personal and ultimately a collective immaturity. Inevitably, most leaders can't measure up to our expectations and let their followers down, though in their still-masked state they may lie and cheat to cover up their mistakes. Followers see all this and accuse their leaders of deception or worse. It's like a failure machine, an endless loop of excessive expectations followed by inauthenticity, shame, and loathing. If left unexamined, the machine will continue to spit out ineffective leaders, and the people they were supposed to lead will continue to feel betrayed and disgusted.

The leaders I met—exemplars in their fields—were nothing like this; the failure machine was not part of the calculus. They believed in and genuinely liked themselves, and seemed to follow their own inner muse. They were good in some things and not in others, but more importantly, they didn't expect themselves to be all knowing. Instead, they surrounded themselves with people who complemented their missing capabilities.

Leaders come in all shapes and personalities, as multiple sources and common wisdom have suggested. In the study by John Zenger and Joseph Folkman referred to earlier, there was wide variability in the competence of great leaders; of 16 identified competencies, no leader had the same four strengths. Building on the strengths one does have is a key to success, as is the building of a strong leadership team.

The people I interviewed were also guided by a sense of self-authority. By this I mean that they know themselves as the author of their own lives; it is not an authority for or over others. It is the same quality that caused Mahatma Gandhi to stand up to the British hierarchy and say, "No more," and that motivated Fred Smith, the founder of Federal Express, to build an extraordinary business when others said it was impossible to compete with the U.S. Postal Service. Self-authority has driven Henry Ford, Madame Curie, Margaret Thatcher, Martin Luther King, and countless other change agents throughout history. It reveals the power and promise of the golden flame that smolders from deep within—a relentless desire to live full and passionate lives directed toward a meaningful cause.

Such leadership has little interest in cultivating dependency. Instead it challenges others to step up and claim their own space. The best leadership, the kind that really matters, encourages us to learn and grow,

> *The best leadership, the kind that really matters, encourages us to learn and grow, to take responsibility for ourselves.*

to take responsibility for ourselves. While remarkable leaders are intent on making their own positive mark in the world, they are equally committed to supporting others to make theirs—and people inevitably respond. That kind of leadership is golden.

The First Remarkable Leader I Met

I met Chauncey Starr in the cafeteria of the Electric Power Research Institute (EPRI) one beautiful autumn day in 2005. More than 30 years earlier, Chauncey saw that technological advancement in the electric utility industry was happening in piecemeal fashion, each company moving the technological needle only modestly. If someone could bring all this effort and financial strength together, he thought, it would be good for the industry and therefore good for the world. The result was EPRI. Energized by Chauncey's ability to harness the talents of people in many different organizations, EPRI has spawned scores of significant advancements in the energy services arena, including ultrasonic cleaning for nuclear fuel, combustion turbine simulators, nuclear waste management, and cable testing, among many others.

One of EPRI's long-standing leaders, Ric Rudman, recommended that I talk with Chauncey. "You have to meet him. He's incredible."

"In what way is he so incredible?" I queried, impressed by the endorsement.

"Just meet him, Keith. You'll see."

It wasn't hard finding Chauncey at the EPRI cafeteria; there aren't many people still in the workforce at age 93. He was slowly walking toward a table when I arrived. I went up to him and introduced myself. He smiled briefly and asked me if I would carry his tray for him. On it was a bowl of soup, nothing more. "At my age, things get a bit heavy," he said somewhat apologetically.

We sat down, and while I prepared my micro-cassette for the interview, he took some food from a sack and in a slow, methodical manner pieced together a Spartan little sandwich. "My doctor tells me I have to watch my cholesterol," he informed me. And, after a pause, he softly asked, "So how can I help you?"

"I'm trying to get to the heart and soul of what great leadership is all about," I eagerly replied. "Ric thought you had a lot to say about the subject."

"I'm not so sure. I really don't see myself as a leader," Chauncey replied.

"Oh," I responded, a bit startled. Here was the person who perhaps more than any other human being has helped shape the modern utility industry. "Then—how do you see yourself?"

"I'm just a guy who likes to solve big problems," he replied.

"And why is that?"

He thought for a moment. "Oh, I don't know. I guess I've always been fascinated by problems. They're interesting to deal with, because you never know the rules of the game until you start playing."

Chauncey talked for a bit about his days as a student, his post-doctoral work at Harvard, his experience as a research assistant at MIT. Then he shared a revealing story about an event in 1943 when the Navy asked him to try to solve the problem of hulls being breached by enemy torpedoes. Chauncey's contribution was finding a way of measuring shockwaves, which ultimately led to significant improvements in hull design. With growing enthusiasm, he went on to tell me about other significant problems he had solved, such as inventing a minesweeper that may have saved hundreds of lives.

Here was a remarkable leader who had played a significant role in helping win WWII, founded and led one of the most important institutions in the electric power industry, and saw himself not as a leader but as a man doing his best to be useful. At the tender age of 93, sitting hunched in his chair without a hint of vanity, Chauncey spoke for two hours about everything that has to do with leadership—yet never once claimed to be a leader himself! While Chauncey demonstrated a feisty personality, that's not what impressed me the most. It was his genuineness and his powerful sense of purpose. He sat with me without pretension or the need to prove himself and shared the story of his adult life, one that was rich with meaning, value, and learning. The power of his presence and his way of expressing himself fully, authentically, and with grace and ease, was the golden flame that stood out for me. And it was the same golden flame I witnessed in others, over and over and over again.

✧

The challenge of embodying a mature expression of leadership is daunting and few achieve it. The problem is not the how-to; numerous books give very useful guidance. The problem is making the commitment to achieving great leadership and then making the necessary internal changes to get there. Said differently, the gap between *knowing* how to be a great leader and *being* one—to actually embodying greatness—is huge, and little is known about how to bridge the two. It's not that we don't understand the goal; the problem is actually getting there, and understanding the reasons why so few leaders do. Why do some people step up to the challenge while most do not? My journey revealed a few answers.

KEY POINTS IN CHAPTER 1

- Confidence in leadership is low and has been for decades.

- Great leadership has a quantum leap impact on organizational performance.

- Our desire for great leadership from others is to some extent an expression of our own unmet needs.

- The key to great leadership is self-authorship—the ability to be the author of one's own life.

- Great leaders invite others to step up and take responsibility for themselves.

CHAPTER 2

---◇---

THE ESSENCE OF REMARKABLE LEADERSHIP

What lies before us and what lies behind us are
small matters compared to what lies within us.
And when we bring what is within out into the
world, miracles happen.

—Henry David Thoreau

To understand the heart and soul of great leadership, we need alternative ways of seeing, ways not ordinarily available to us in our daily lives. We must look beyond or beneath our surface words and actions to see the qualities that give rise to them. We need to soften our eyes, quiet the mind, and sense from a different place of knowing. It was Rumi, the Persian poet, who said:

When physical vision has transcended space,
another sky opens up to the eyes of the soul.[1]

When I met the remarkable leaders referred to in this book, I didn't know what I would find. I wasn't looking for any particular answer. Mostly, I was deeply curious. At the same time, I admitted to myself a yearning to know that such people were really out there, that my search was not quixotic. And as I looked at the larger truth of my journey, I realized that I was aching for the leader within me to emerge from hiding and reveal itself.

One Such Leader

Bannus Hudson met me in the hallway of his unimposing office building in Concord, California. Five years now as CEO of BevMo, the rapidly growing beverage retailer, he greeted me with warmth and a reserve that bespoke his Midwestern background.

"Can I get you anything?" he offered.

"A bit of water would be great," I replied.

He escorted me to his office; noticeably small and simply adorned with a couple of paintings and plenty of blank wall space. I was reminded anew that so many of the leaders I met worked in unassuming surroundings—this one especially so.

Up until 20 years ago, Bannus's business history was solid but hardly the stuff of legends. He had moved up the Proctor & Gamble corporate ladder, became head of one of its largest manufacturing operations, and then one day was offered the chance to run a 25-store retail operation with a solid business model and potential for growth. That company was LensCrafters, and in 1987 Bannus became its CEO.

LensCrafters was created to provide one-stop shopping for quality eyeglasses. At the time, most eyeglasses were sold at high prices and with only modest selections by ophthalmologists as an add-on business to their professional services. The founders of LensCrafters thought that these sales should be the core business of a retail store, with lower costs achieved through higher volume. Under Bannus's leadership, the idea took off and in less than ten years the company had grown to more than 800 stores.

"So, how can I help you?" Bannus asked with quiet dignity, comfortable and calm in his trim, middle-aged body.

I started with a thank you and a bit of my own history. He listened intently, offering an occasional smile or a nod, thoughtfully taking in my story.

"Leadership is a big interest of mine," he said. "I think about it often."

"In what way?" I replied, welcoming his lead.

"Well, I think I'm a pretty good leader at this stage in my life," he said unabashedly. "I wasn't always."

"Was there a turning point for you?"

"Yes, there was..." And so it began. What was so telling about Bannus, and so many of the leaders I met, is the ease with which he spoke about life and the sense that I got from his body language, tone, and demeanor that here is a man who is comfortable in his skin. He didn't apologize for the way he had been before the turning point (you will hear about it later in the book), nor did he attach monumental significance to the intervention that caused it. He simply saw himself as a guy on a journey of learning, who committed himself to adding value to the people around him.

We talked for another two hours, our conversation exploring the contours of his professional life—what he's experienced, what he's observed, how he makes sense of himself. One particular moment stood out for me as he talked about BevMo.

"I saw a company with great potential but also in disarray," he said in recalling his decision to take the job. "The founders had a great idea but weren't able to get everyone rowing in the same direction. I observed for a while and offered a simple strategy for helping the company get to the other side."

Bannus spoke in great detail about the strategy and its critical role in the company's success, both now and in the future. The strategy was simple, elegant, and compelling, focusing on the centrality of the customer experience. But more important than the details of this strategy was the way in which he described it. His eyes were clear and his demeanor was quiet and direct. He never fidgeted. He would often pause as he took his time to speak. It was not so much that his words were measured, for they flowed easily; it was the depth of his thoughtfulness. He took great care in making sure that I understood precisely what he was saying.

And when he spoke of the importance of the company's culture, his eyes lit up, for he knew that this was the legacy he would someday leave behind. "What I am most proud of," he said, "is that I have implanted a powerful customer-service orientation in the company. It is without a doubt our sustainable competitive advantage."

Like all the great leaders I met, he knew that values and culture are more than ideas—they must become the company's heart and soul to have any lasting meaning and impact. And that starts with wise leadership and how leaders conduct themselves.

As we talked, it became evident that Bannus Hudson was clear about who he was and who he was not, someone with a clear sense of direction and solid in his sense of self. This solidity showed less in the words he spoke than in the way he spoke them. His voice was calm and soft-spoken. His gaze was sure and yet without being uncomfortably penetrating. And when I offered my responses and thoughts, he let them in and considered their significance. His inner essence and inner clarity had a magnetic quality that drew me in.

Gravitas is a good word for this. When people have strong gravitas, they are centered, grounded, clear, a force to be reckoned with. They carry the weight of their inner certainty, and it shows not so much in what you see but what you feel about them. This feeling goes well beyond personality. It lies much deeper.

Some management analysts claim that only certain types of personalities (e.g., charismatic, oratorical, entrepreneurial, "driver") are suited for leadership. I have my doubts. So does business guru Jim Collins, who points out in his book *Good to Great* that many of the most successful companies, at least those that have moved from being good in their industry to being the best, tend to be run by uncharismatic, unassuming leaders. In my way of reading Collins' description, instead they had *gravitas*—the powerful pull of their core convictions.

To identify the leadership gene in a particular personality is a wild goose chase. In my meetings with remarkable leaders, I encountered extraordinarily diverse personality types and behavioral styles. Everyone I spoke with seemed to have their own unique style: Some were quiet and reserved, and some were slow and deliberate. Some were stoic while others were effusive. Still others were playful and boisterous. They all touched me deeply, not from what they showed on the surface but from what emanated from within.

At the same time, certain patterns and commonalities were clearly evident. In fact, a content analysis of the interview transcripts revealed seven consistent attributes, none of which was especially surprising:

The 7 Consistent Attributes	
Vision	The capacity to see the big picture and what might be possible
A commitment to learning	Humility in the face of what isn't known, but also an eagerness to push the boundaries
Principle-driven	Decisions and actions motivated not by personal vanity but by core values
A desire to be the best	A hunger beyond competitiveness to perform at the highest possible level
An appetite to challenge the status quo	An innate drive to challenge the status quo
A commitment to service	The needs of others and the larger community are always considered
Empowering others	Authentic respect and care for the well-being and success of others[2]

Similar attributes have been written about in most leadership books of the past 30 years and espoused by nearly every leadership expert in the Western world.[3] Devoting another book to discussing them would be redundant. But this only proves my point. How is it that we can know and teach these attributes so thoroughly, and yet we are no better today than we ever were at producing exceptional, even competent, leaders?

I think the reasons are twofold: The first is that we too often imagine that *studying* the art and science of great leadership will make us great leaders. Countless books and thousands of leadership trainings have proven otherwise. The second reason is that we just aren't looking deeply enough for answers. Yes, those seven attributes of superior leadership appear to differentiate those I interviewed from the countless others in similar positions, but if it's a formula that can't be duplicated, then where does that leave us? Unless we can bring those attributes to life, they just stare back at us like fish on a plate. This tells me that there is something more elusive about the process of becoming a great leader than intellectual understanding.

And so I sought to know what lives behind these noble characteristics. Why do they show up so powerfully in some leaders and not at all in others? What causes them to show up in the first place? Is there something deeper that ties these characteristics together, a pattern that reveals the elusive secret formula? What am I sensing in the people I interviewed that cannot be explained by over-worn references to courage, determination, caring, and the like?

The answers to these questions eventually revealed themselves; in meeting with so many great leaders, I began to understand the lessons that had eluded my grasp for so long. In essence, what I distilled from these individuals is that they are remarkable not just for what they do or how they conduct themselves in business but for *how they show up in life*. They were *present*. They were *secure*. They were *at peace with themselves*. With few exceptions I felt touched by these leaders—by their humanity, their resolve, and their delightful openness to explore. My search for precise words seems unable to fully describe the feeling I had when in their company. It wasn't specific leadership qualities as much as the unseen forces that gave rise to those qualities. The closest I can come to capturing this experience is the notion of self-authorship—each of them resonated with an authenticity that felt rooted in a deep connection with self.

> *...they are remarkable not just for what they do or how they conduct themselves in business but for how they show up in life.*

I attended a memorial service a few months ago. Close friends of our family had just lost one of their daughters, Morgan, who suffered from numerous handicaps in her too-short life. As the rabbi rose, all stood in quiet anticipation. The temple was heavy with grief. The loss of a child is hard to witness, and, for the parents, extraordinarily painful to bear. The rabbi was about to speak when he suddenly paused. It was as if he became aware that he wasn't quite ready, that he was about to go through the motions of conducting the service when much more was needed. He waited... and waited. I could see that he was bringing himself completely to the present, becoming full with his own feelings about the loss and enveloping the room with his love. Then, finally, he spoke, and his humanity was tangible. In that simple act of being fully there, we felt him, one another, and the tenderness of the moment.

The rabbi's words seemed to give all of us permission to bring our deepest selves forward as the service kept calling forth a powerful sense of genuine expression. One person after another stepped up to the podium and spoke purely from the heart. One of the most memorable moments occurred when my former wife, Tina, got up to speak. She said a few words and then talked about a song that had been playing in her head while reflecting on the loss of Morgan. It was a famous folk song called "Today," and she explained that it reminded her of how Morgan was a testimony to the powerful effect of living in the moment. That was Morgan's gift—living every day as if tomorrow might never be.

As Tina began to sing the song her voice began to crack, so much so that she could barely continue. Feeling the depth of her emotion, I joined in to let her know she wasn't alone. My teenage son, forgetting thoughts of embarrassment, started singing as well, and one by one everyone who knew the song sang it, loud and clear. The effect was extraordinary, and connected us all.

Magical moments happen when people break through the patterns and routines of daily life and speak their truths. Among the leaders I talked with, that authenticity showed up less in their actual words than in the way they gave voice to those words. It showed up not so much in the content but in how their body conveyed the message. *I concluded that great leadership has something—and perhaps everything—to do with being in touch with one's inner wisdom.* The lives of great leaders make a difference because they're fueled by purpose and meaning, and at a level that stands out from most others.

> *Great leadership has something—and perhaps everything—to do with inner wisdom.*

In making that difference they've learned to implicitly trust themselves. Their hand is firmly on the tiller of their own life. They are living the spirit of leadership and authenticity called forth in William Ernest Henley's poem, *Invictus:*

OUT of the night that covers me,
Black as the Pit from pole to pole,
I thank whatever gods may be
For my unconquerable soul.

In the fell clutch of circumstance
I have not winced nor cried aloud.
Under the bludgeonings of chance
My head is bloody, but unbowed.

Beyond this place of wrath and tears
Looms but the Horror of the shade,
And yet the menace of the years
Finds, and shall find, me unafraid.

It matters not how strait the gate,
How charged with punishments the scroll,
I am the master of my fate:
I am the captain of my soul.

Here is the stirring of the deep quality that distinguishes remarkable leaders from the rest of us. It is the power of connecting with and heeding the directions of one's own internal guidance system. That sense of self-authorship, of being one's own captain and willing to risk it all, is what we're seeing and feeling when moved to say about someone, "Now, there is a great leader."

> *Remarkable leaders are remarkable less for their deeds than for the way they "show up" in life.*

After months of meetings with such remarkable people, I was able to see that each one's life was directed by the urgings of their heart and soul. Seneca, in *Letters from a Stoic*, said it beautifully:

> *A man's ideal state is realized when he has fulfilled the purpose for which he is born. And what is it that reason demands of him? Something very easy—that he live in accordance with his own nature.[4]*

In exploring this notion of following one's own inner guidance system, I have come to identify three specific characteristics that seem to give rise to all the other behaviors we associate with great leadership:

✓ **A Clear Inner Compass.** Remarkable leaders have an unerring sense of their own true north. This steady inner compass reflects a clear vision and sense of purpose, served by a willingness to stay the course regardless of obstacles and distractions.

✓ **A Powerful Inner Anchor.** The leaders I met have a powerful set of values—a sense of right and wrong—that gives them inner peace and engenders trust from others. They are also anchored in a core belief that the job of a leader is to create the conditions that allow others to achieve their highest potential.

✓ **A Rock-Solid Sense of Self.** Remarkable leaders have a strong sense of self-esteem rooted in an awareness of their true gifts. They accept themselves fully and aren't threatened by those with differing gifts. Self-acceptance allows great leaders to admit their mistakes and shortcomings, to learn from the people around them, and to step gracefully through their own pitfalls.

Let's consider briefly these three qualities. For example, where does vision come from? An idea? A belief? Both are crucial, but they are not the true source. I now believe that powerful vision comes from the well of deep purpose. No great leader has a vision without a deep sense of personal purpose, a knowing of their place in the world. Too often, leadership workshops ask participants to develop their own vision, which they spend (too little) time doing. Then they read it out loud and ask others for feedback. The problem is that such an exercise fails to recognize that vision doesn't come from thinking or an orderly five-step process. It comes from a place inside that reaches beyond the intellect. Moreover, a unique and powerful vision isn't served by feedback but by authenticity; it must be true to itself, not to others. It is a deep and powerful sense of purpose that gives rise to vision, conviction, drive, and determination, all qualities that we easily and quickly identify in great leaders.

Where does integrity come from? Not from an idea or a belief in the value of values, but from *living* one's values. Great leaders resonate with an inner knowing that the riches that matter are those that come from a life lived with integrity. They don't *have* values; they *are* their values. And it is from this powerful anchor of values that courage, trustworthiness, and consistency in thought and deed arise, all qualities that define great leadership.

And finally, where does risk-taking or courage come from? Not from an idea or a belief in its value or importance. It comes from knowing that, no matter what happens, you are okay inside. People with strong self-esteem are willing to make mistakes because failure doesn't cause them to question who they are. Instead it teaches them something new and important to learn. You can't teach this in a classroom or come to it from reading a book. That rock-solid sense of self is earned through years of excavating one's inner landscape—facing down one's inner demons and coming out the better for it. Achieving it gives rise to humility, grace, openness to other opinions, a commitment to diversity, the ability to delegate and to surround oneself with a strong team, and a never-ending journey of growth and learning.

In short, all of the qualities we admire in great leaders emerge out of three foundational forces: a clear inner compass, a powerful anchor of values, and a rock solid sense of self. When all of these forces are alive in people, they naturally manifest the qualities we associate with great leadership: powerful personal presence without pushiness; sureness without arrogance; and humility that allows for extraordinary accomplishment without hubris or false pride. These characteristics help describe the phenomenon of *self-authorship*—that singular culminating expression of those who have achieved leadership mastery by drawing from resources that are both invisible to the eye and eternal. Perhaps the reason why we don't develop great leadership in the world or in ourselves is that we simply aren't looking deep enough for its source.

Seeing these forces in each of the leaders I met was profoundly inspiring, leading me to look closely at my own self-identity and what I bring to the world. Time and time again I would ask myself, *"Who am I?" "What is my purpose?" "What is my destination in life and in work?" "What do I care so deeply about that I am willing to give up everything for?" "What are my triggers to judgment or anger?" "How do I maintain inner solidity when everything around me is crumbling?"* These are not idle musings. They are some of the questions that great leaders keep asking themselves, not so much for personal gain but so that they can bring their gifts more fully to the world around them.

Throughout this book, you will see that these three meta-attributes—an *inner compass*, a *powerful anchor*, and a *solid sense of self*—occupy ground zero of our inquiry. In the chapters that follow, you will learn from the leaders I met, and also from others whose experiences offer additional insights, how these meta-attributes shape and give rise to the qualities of leadership that we yearn for in our leaders and that we seek within ourselves in nurturing our own self-authorship. Consider asking yourselves the kinds of questions noted above. It is in the asking that you will go deeper and find the essence of who you are and who you might become, and in so doing, you will locate a glowing spark of leadership within you and coax that spark into a brilliant, golden flame.

KEY POINTS IN CHAPTER 2

- There is no correlation between personality and great leadership.

- There is a direct correlation between inner strength or "gravity" and remarkable leadership.

- Knowing the competencies of great leaders will not help someone become a great leader.

- There is a deeper set of hard earned qualities that naturally give rise to the competencies of great leadership. They are:
    - Having a clear and powerful inner compass
    - Being anchored in ones values
    - Having a rock solid sense of self

CHAPTER 3

---◇---

THE COMPASS OF PURPOSE

*When you know who you are; when your mission
is clear and you burn with the inner fire of
unbreakable will; no cold can touch your heart;
no deluge can dampen your purpose. You know
that you are alive.*

—Chief Seattle

Henry Wadsworth Longfellow wrote a Psalm in the mid 19th century whose lines have been haunting me ever since I read them 15 years ago. He said,

> Lives of great men all remind us
> We can make our lives sublime,
> And, departing, leave behind us
> Footprints on the sands of time.[1]

These lines challenge me with questions: *What footprint am I leaving? What will my legacy be?*

In truth, I don't yet know the answer. I get glimpses of my potential, but too often I'm aware of how ordinary I feel as I struggle to find grace in the many moments of my day-to-day activities. I feel ordinary when I get angry with my teenage son. I feel ordinary when I'm not loving and present with the people closest to me. I feel ordinary in those moments when the world seems full of life but all I experience inside is deadness.

If I died tomorrow, will others come to my funeral? What will they say about the meaning of my life? On my 50th birthday, my ex-wife Tina threw me a wonderful party with more than 60 guests. It was a day rich with joy, celebration, and ritual. At one point, with my encouragement, she asked the guests to share what impact I'd had in their lives. In perhaps a preview of my funeral, many stepped forward.

A few said they were touched by my belief in them. Some thanked me for mentoring them and being a powerful role model for living life with integrity and open-heartedness. Several shared how I helped guide them to be leaders. Still others appreciated my efforts to be honest with both them and myself. I felt profoundly grateful knowing I'd had an impact, that I had made a difference in their lives. And yet I also wondered whether these warm remembrances were what I was meant for, or if there was still more in store for me before my life's end. And then, as the sweet fragrance of their generous feedback lingered, I had a brief moment of awakening and awareness that has stayed with me ever since: When my flame goes out, I want to have run out of fuel, to have used up every ounce. I want to know my purpose and to have fulfilled it—completely and wholeheartedly.

Few people in Western society have a firm grasp on their purpose in life. We are enthralled with celebrity and conquest and with media images of what constitutes "success." In setting our sights on material goals, we seldom stop and ask ourselves, *Why am I here? What is my true calling?* Without answers to these questions, we drift from job to job and career to career, cobbling together a life we hope is worth living, measuring success in outward terms. Like a peacock displaying its tail, we find gratification in showing the world how successful we are. *Look at what I own! Look at what I've done!* But we seldom feel satisfied. We perceive beauty when it's obvious but completely miss the inner beauty that's more enduring.

The older I get, the more I recognize that my early definitions of success now ring hollow. Over time something deeper began to stir in me, a yearning, a sense of knowing, that there is more to the measure of one's life. It is this knowledge of deeper purpose—a clear and powerful inner compass—that distinguishes great leaders and shows them true north.

In the Christian world, priests and ministers speak of their vocation or "calling," as if called to serve God's purpose. At a more secular level, I once heard it said that *a calling is when one's greatest joy meets the world's greatest need.* The idea is that we are here on this earth for a purpose, and to live that purpose yields the greatest value for oneself and for the world. In his book *The World Behind the World*, mythologist-storyteller Michael Meade writes, "The old idea was that each person has a proportion of achievement to accomplish in one lifetime and each a share of service to be offered up. We live most fully when living out both energies in proportion to the innate shape of our soul."[2] This is what I experienced in the presence of each of the leaders I met in my journey. They are each living out their soul's purpose, without a hint of self-importance *or* apology. Here are just a few examples:

✓ For Chauncey Starr, profiled in the previous chapter, it means keeping the lights on—making electricity safe, universally available, and inexpensive throughout the world.

✓ For Charles Garcia, founder and leader of The Sterling Financial Group, one of the country's fastest-growing Hispanic-led financial services organization, it's about helping Hispanics live a better life and inspiring all peoples to find their leadership within.

✓ For Paul Centenari, the co-owner of Atlas Container Corporation, it is dedicating himself to the belief that ordinary people can do extraordinary things when given the tools to make their own decisions.

✓ For Scott Johnson, founder of the Myelin Repair Foundation, it is changing the way we approach medical research and stretching our understanding of and ability to treat multiple sclerosis.

✓ For Mimi Silbert, founder and CEO of The Delancey Street Foundation, it is dedicating her life to the belief that former criminals and addicts can have a full and healthy life if they live in a community where they are needed, treated with dignity, and supported to take responsibility for their own lives.

Such passion to make a difference was palpable in every interview I had. I left each meeting inspired, and inevitably returning to the question, *Who am I in this world?* In a younger version of myself, such thoughts were displaced by my ambition to succeed, my desire for comfort and having "nice stuff," and my unconscious drive to prove to my father that I was worthy. The leaders on my journey saw beyond all that. Directly or indirectly, everything they did "served"—either to meet a specific need or to meet their soul's desire—and it didn't matter whether they led profit-driven or nonprofit organizations.

> *A calling is when one's greatest joy meets the world's greatest need.*

I recently attended a monthly meeting of CEOs who gather to discuss the challenges they are facing. In this particular meeting, all but one was struggling in some significant way. As I listened to their stories, it became clear that many of them lacked a clear inner compass telling them what to do with their lives and their talents. One CEO was leading a company that, while relentlessly opportunistic, lacked a core philosophy to guide its choices. This orientation reflected the founders' behavior, perpetuated by a management team that was unwilling to confront the pattern. A second CEO faced the prospect of his company being acquired, knew that this violated his own inner compass, but was unwilling to come out and say so. A third CEO admitted he hadn't followed his soul's desire and now, at middle age, faced a major crossroads—to risk change or to endlessly tread water.

As we talked about their challenges, I suggested that in each situation, they were either unclear about their own inner compass or they knew where it pointed but weren't following its direction. They acknowledged this possibility but felt there was too much at stake. I said that I thought the opposite was true: "The greater risk is in not following your own inner guidance system. You all know what the right choice is; you are just unwilling to make it." I could sense their discomfort; it was a truth that they didn't want to hear.

The one exception in this group didn't suffer from lack of clarity. He knew his company and its value to the world, and he knew exactly where he wanted to take it. In contrast to the others, stifled by anxiety, depression, or confusion, this man was grounded and composed—a solidity that reflected a sense of inner knowing.

During lunch, he revealed to me that, "I don't always know the right thing to do for my company, and there are times I'm just as uncertain as the next person. But the difference is that I know who I am, I know fundamentally where I'm going, and I know my purpose. With those as my guide, decisions come much more easily." In those precious few words, he echoed what I heard from nearly all of the remarkable leaders I discuss in this book. And he also reminded me that many of these people had little interest in the fact that they were "leaders." I've known many ambitious leaders who are enamored with themselves, but those I focus on seemed indifferent to—and even uncomfortable with—their position "at the top." Their focus was on their purpose, their lives dedicated to a cause.

Guided by a Deep Purpose

Jerry Jampolsky is one such leader. He is former executive director of the Center for Attitudinal Healing (now called the CorStone Center), which he co-founded with his wife Diane Circinione in 1975. At the heart of the Center's philosophy and work is a belief that we have the power to choose our attitude in any given moment, regardless of the circumstances, and that everyone can cultivate emotional resilience in the face of challenge, crisis, and conflict.

Jerry has won numerous honors in his life, and at age 83 he remains robust and active, still working hard for the cause of healing. He has written or co-written eight books on the subject of personal growth and inner healing, each of which has the same core message: To live a life of satisfaction and fulfillment, find it in your heart to love and to forgive others.

In the early summer of 2006, Jerry invited me to visit him in Sausalito on his houseboat overlooking the San Francisco Bay. My first assumption was that this was a second home, or his office, or an eccentric getaway. I was wrong on all counts. The modest, bobbing, two-bedroom structure *was* his primary residence. As I rang the doorbell, I wondered to myself (embarrassed now to admit it) how remarkable could this man be if he couldn't afford a fancier place than this?

The door opened and an elderly man greeted me, wearing only a pair of khaki shorts—no shirt or shoes. He smiled warmly. "Welcome," he said. "May I give you a hug?" "Sure," I responded, always open to a hug, and he embraced me, not in the way that most men do—a quick, hunched-over, shoulder-touching, make-sure-we-don't-get-too-close, let's-smack-each-other-on-the-back-quickly-and-get-this-over-with kind of hug. It was a warm, full-body embrace that lasted quite a few seconds. The greeting, the setting, and how he showed up told me I was in for something unusual, and Jerry did not disappoint. Indeed, his presence and his message ended up challenging me to change my life.

His houseboat was modestly adorned with pictures, sculptures, and artifacts that all spoke to peace and simplicity. He led me to his living room, the perimeter of which was all glass, allowing for a gorgeous view of the Bay. After taking our seats, he asked, "So what can I do for you?" I reminded him of the purpose of our visit and began in my usual fashion by asking him about his leadership style. He responded just like Chauncey Starr had. "I don't think of myself as a leader."

"You don't?" I queried.

"No, not really."

"So what do you think of when you think about yourself?"

He thought for a moment and then replied, "I think about how I can make a bigger difference in people's lives."

This one little response said it all. When I asked him to tell me what inspired him to found the Center for Attitudinal Healing, he shared this story:

It was 1975. I had a good reputation in Marin County as a top psychiatrist. I was also very involved in hypnosis and other new modalities of treatment. One day I was making my rounds at the UC-Berkeley Medical Center when I overheard a 7-year-old kid with terminal cancer ask the oncologist, "What is it like to die?" Clearly uncomfortable, the oncologist changed the subject. I thought to myself, 'Where do kids go when they want to talk to somebody about things like this? Who will have an honest conversation with them?' The next day I decided to get some kids together and help them help each other—to create a kind of spiritual/psychological support group. I explained that I was going to deal with them as if they were my equal. I would share my thoughts and invite them to share theirs. If they didn't like that, maybe we wouldn't do it. But they liked the idea.

Six weeks later the kids decided to keep going. As time went on we began seeing more people. I had some very clear guidance that these kids were wise spirits in young bodies, quickly teaching me another way of looking at life and at death, of seeing one's purpose.

Soon I was moved to ask Jerry again about what makes him a great leader. His response was telling:

I realize that other people look at me as a leader or a visionary, but I don't think of myself that way. I've always had a very active imagination, and I think when you have an active imagination and you come with a higher sense of purpose and a feeling that the most important thing in

*the world is not achieving but how to get along with and
love each other, you end up inspiring people. My wife and
I are known for that, not by setting ourselves up as a
shining example but by readily sharing our dirty linen. In
our work with others, we humanize ourselves.*

"So if you don't consider yourself a leader," I said, "how do you think
of yourself?"

Radiating warmth and ease, he replied without hesitation, "As a child
of God, doing my best to listen to an inner voice telling me what to think,
say, and do."

Then it hit me: Rarely did I listen to my inner voice. My mind was
usually focused on other things—accomplishing a task, checking off the
next thing on my list. I squirmed in my chair, all too aware that I had much
to learn. Jerry continued.

"I think we make decisions based on either fear or love, and I think
we make much better decisions when we base them on love. Then we can
get beyond what we would consider our normal limitations."

After sitting with Jerry for only a short time, his sense of purpose had
come through to me loud and clear. Through his words, and equally
through his demeanor, I could feel the purity of that purpose. What
followed told me even more about his conviction.

Soon after reading The Course of Miracles[3] *and embracing
the power and potency of love and forgiveness in our
lives, I had some guidance not to charge any more money
for helping people.* [By "guidance," I knew that he wasn't
referring to another person.] *After about two years I ran
out of money and my secretary came in and said, "I don't
know how to tell you this, but you've got all these bills
and you can't pay them and I think you ought to go see a
psychiatrist." At around that same time, Orson Beane, a
well-known actor known to have had alcohol problems,
was on the Johnny Carson show. In response to a question*

by Johnny, essentially asking him, "What's new in your life?" Orson pulled out the first book I had written, held it up in front of the camera to millions of viewers, and said, "This book saved my life."

All of a sudden people were paying me money to give lectures. Over time more than 130 Centers for Attitudinal Healing were set up all over the world. I believe that being a good leader is really about being a good follower. When you listen to that inner voice and follow it [so that's what he meant by "guidance"], *you become a powerful magnet for others who say, ' I want some of that inner peace, too. How do I find it?'*

I wish that every reader of this book could have been there with Jerry at this moment, for what I experienced was a man who understood something deep and profound—that to live life fully, one has to let go of ego-driven concerns and give their love away to others. He wasn't concerned with material wealth. He cared about spiritual, social, and emotional health, and it was powerfully represented in his bearing, his effusive nature, and the modest way he lived.

In contrast, I am reminded of the countless times when I've read or heard the following description of someone: "He's worth $___ dollars." It reflects our society's relentless penchant to measure a person's value in dollars and cents. Jerry clearly didn't see his own worth in this way and was completely at peace with that.

As I kept listening to this remarkable man, I couldn't help reflecting on my own life. While the work I was doing felt purpose-driven—I have dedicated my life to helping organizations become extraordinary both in their performance and in the way people work together—I didn't feel very good about my work at the moment. I did not feel fulfilled. I decided to confide in this man, sensing that he had much to offer me.

"Jerry, can we stop here for a moment."

He nodded.

"What you are saying moves me to admit that sometimes I don't feel like I'm fully present with my clients, that I'm working from my head and not my heart. I sometimes feel distant, disconnected, not fully there." I surprised myself with this candor.

His response was simple. "Well, it seems to me you're acting from some limiting beliefs."

"What limiting beliefs?" I asked, feeling both tentative and eager.

"I'm not sure yet. Maybe you're afraid to fully embrace that your love for others is all that matters."

I struggled with his feedback. It sounded, well, like pabulum. "I must tell you," I said, squirming again in my chair, "that I'm really resisting what you're saying."

"I know," he said calmly. After a pause he asked, "What are you resisting?"

"I'm not sure," I replied. "Maybe I don't want to hear it because if it's true, I have to admit that I'm not living fully what I preach."

As these disturbing words tumbled out of my mouth, I felt exposed, and yet before a feeling of shame enveloped me, he simply nodded, smiled warmly, and said, "It's okay." In that one simple gesture, all of who he was came to the fore—a man committed to unconditional love. I felt it deeply, and as this feeling washed over me, I allowed myself to also feel the truth of what I was facing.

We get feedback from the world all the time, whether or not we want to admit or acknowledge it. For example, when a person stares at us as we cut into a line or when someone's silence has a feeling of anger in it. In these ways feedback is ever present. More rare is the kind of feedback when a person directly says, "I'd like to tell you how your behavior impacted me." I am reminded that we rarely let that feedback in. When we do, it's often on a cognitive level, which doesn't truly penetrate. By virtue of his loving embrace, my own self-awareness, and the honesty between us, Jerry's feedback on the potential impact of limiting beliefs in my life *did* penetrate, and I could feel motivated to face myself more fully.

And so it went. For the next hour we discussed the way I'd been living my life. I confided in him the struggles I'd been having in my work and with my family, and throughout our talk he lovingly reflected my thoughts back to me. I started to finally understand the source of my anguish—I was making too many choices from my ego and not from my heart. I was living from analysis and intellect and either uncomfortable or afraid to live in my heart. As he kept offering the possibility of making the leap to embrace more of what I knew I was capable of, I kept asking myself, "Could it be so simple?"

Yes, it could. But it wasn't easy to fully own the lessons before me. I would have to let go of the belief that material things matter and that success meant demonstrating that I was capable, smart, and special. I would have to face the fears that prevented me from expressing my deeper feelings and beliefs no matter what they were. These inner patterns of conditioning (or *attachment*, to use a Buddhist expression) had not been apparent to me; they dwelled in the crevices of my unconscious. But now they were being exposed in full view through Jerry's particular and powerful perspective on what it means to live a meaningful life.

I asked him how he felt about spending so much time on my challenges and not his leadership. He smiled and said, "It doesn't matter. Let's just be present with what is. Anyway, this *is* my work, and now you get to experience it rather than us talking about it."

Jerry was in his element, not talking about his purpose but being it. This embodiment of deep purpose was palpable in most of the leaders I met in my journey. And in almost all cases, their purpose was selfless; much like the message Jerry was championing—to live a life of love. Many books have been written on the subject of servant-leadership, and each tells the same tale. And yet it's difficult to accurately convey the experience of being with such people who, on the face of it, seem no different than anyone at the top of his or her profession or organization—they are all

> *What makes these leaders so special is that their personal achievement meant so little to them. Their satisfaction comes from serving a larger purpose.*

remarkable achievers. What makes these leaders so special is that their personal achievement meant so little to them. Their satisfaction comes from serving a larger sense of purpose.

Trapped Inside Ourselves

My interview with Jerry resonated for quite a while as I questioned the depth of my own purpose. Would I, like Jerry, forego two years of income in service to something bigger than me, trusting that somehow I would get whatever I needed? Could my ego overcome its conditioned desire for status, achievement, and creature comfort? Although I have a powerful yearning to make a difference in the world, I sometimes wonder how much of this desire is driven by my ego to fulfill some sense of duty or to prove to my parents and to the world that I'm worthy. Sometimes I feel trapped, and I know I'm not alone. Rare is the person who has freed himself from the bondage of his ego and committed to a life of purpose and passion.

An old Japanese proverb says, "The gods only laugh when men pray to them for wealth." Ambitious leaders pray for wealth, for glory, for position and self-aggrandizing power. Remarkable leaders pray for the opportunity to serve well. The story of King Midas is instructive. Like many, Midas believed that if only he were rich, he would be happy. So he made a pact with the gods that everything he touched would turn to gold. The deal ends in misery, however, as the food in his mouth and the wine on his palate turn to gold before he can swallow them. The final blow: his daughter turns to gold as he embraces her. He begs the gods to take his gift away. First amused and then impressed that Midas' learning and contrition were genuine, the gods granted his request as Midas vowed to seek riches in the simpler things in life. To great leaders, the power of these "simpler things" is vital to living one's purpose. On one's inner compass they are part of true north.

In his book, *The Soul's Code*,[4] James Hillman spoke powerfully and eloquently on the subject of purpose and the soul, describing the soul as having its own intentions that are imprinted within each of us. Like many other spiritually guided psychologists, he believes that much of our psychological distress stems less from early childhood experiences and more from not heeding our soul's deepest calling. Hillman illustrates his theory with many examples of petulant children who eventually became masters of their art. Among them was the great violinist Yehudi Menuhin, who reputedly as a child of four was given the gift of his first violin. Upon seeing it, he immediately threw it on the ground, smashing it to bits. His parents, awestruck by the act, soon learned that young Yehudi rejected the gift because it was not a Stradivarius. Was this an entitled child acting out or a future genius whose deepest calling demanded an instrument to match his capacity for brilliance? Hillman believes it's the latter, and that each person's soul is encoded with such a purpose, accessible at a very young age.

And so getting in touch with this innate longing, whatever the challenge to getting there, will have a powerful impact on the decisions we make, the work we do, and what we manifest in the world. For a leader, being in touch with one's purpose clarifies the playing field. It enables them to know when to say "Yes" and, equally important, when to say "No." In this way, clarity of purpose becomes a powerful compass for navigating life. In a world where there is enormous pressure to perform and to outpace the competition, this clarity is golden. Great leaders learn how to focus themselves and their organization so that everyone knows where true north is and pulls their oars in the same direction. Their sense of purpose is so potent that achieving its mission feels like a *fait accompli*.

> *Great leaders learn how to focus themselves and their organization so that everyone knows where true north is.*

What Motivates Us

It's often true that leaders reach their position because they drive themselves there. Research shows that most CEOs have a strong need for power and influence and seek positions that allow them to fulfill these needs. This is no less true for remarkable leaders, yet David McClelland's distinction between the need for personalized versus socialized power is particularly instructive. In building a comprehensive profound body of research on what motivates people, the late psychological theorist found that all of us have some combination of three primary needs or motives: the need for *achievement,* the need for *affiliation,* and the need for *power* or *influence.* These three motives account for roughly 95 percent of all human behavior in social situations. McClelland made a compelling case that most human behavior can be explained in terms of how we go about meeting these needs. Moreover, each of us could be said to have a unique motive signature or profile that represents the degree to which these needs live within us.

Not surprisingly, CEOs typically have a much stronger need for power than the average person. What is interesting, though, is how that need for power is expressed. People who have a high need for personalized power, for example, tend to see the world as a win-lose game. Survival of the fittest is their credo and they do whatever it takes to get ahead. They tend to like power for themselves and for its own sake and so they care about their image, like to show off their power, and tend to act in self-aggrandizing ways. In contrast, people who have a high need for socialized power tend to exercise power and influence for the sake of others. Their desire is to use power for the betterment of the whole and not for themselves. They seek win-win solutions to conflict and effectively suppress their inner need for control and domination, knowing that it will not be to the benefit of all.

These two faces of power are especially important to our exploration because power and leadership are inextricably intertwined. Leadership is a game of power and influence. All leaders need to use power, but those who use it primarily for themselves garner little respect from others. The oft-quoted phrase "power corrupts and absolute power corrupts absolutely" speaks to the darker side of such misuse. The other face of power has a life-affirming nature, driven by a deep desire to make a positive difference. Those who use it for the good of all and operate from a purpose larger than themselves tend to be the extraordinary ones. Indeed, through study after study, McClelland found that leaders who exercise socialized power tend to be much more effective in their organizational role than their personalized-power counterparts.[5]

McClelland's findings rang true for the leaders I met. They didn't have the drive to control in quite the same way as other leaders. Few were enamored with power and position, and did not seek it for its own sake (although at one time in their lives they might have). The power they now desired was the power to make a meaningful impact in the world. Here are just a few examples:

Andrea Youngdahl, the head of the Department of Human Services in Oakland:

"My work is about trying to make the world better, the community better, and society better. Everything I've done focuses not on my career, not on my staff members' careers, and not on my management, but on who we serve and how we can make the best servants."

Kartar Singh Khalsa, the CEO of Golden Temple Foods:

"Whatever you do in life—your career, business, whatever it is— somehow it starts from a place of love, not fear. It comes not out of what might happen if I don't do this or what my parents might think, but from a feeling of connection with your destiny. God gives you gifts. You come in with these gifts. It's your responsibility and challenge to use those gifts to the highest and greatest potential in this life."

Joseph Jaworski, CEO of Generon Consulting:

"I feel that there's an element of destiny here for me. I feel deeply about the importance of purpose in life and discovering that purpose. It's like rocket fuel when you click into it."

Chris Chavez, CEO of Advanced Neuromodulation Systems:

"I often tell people that leadership is a privilege, an honor. It's not something that you should aspire to for your own self-serving ends. To lead means you have to have a destiny, a purpose, a mission. You have to know where you're going. Implicit in leadership is the idea that you are pursuing something that's worthy of pursuit. And I believe to my core, and I believe the people in this organization believe to their core, that such pursuit will have a profound impact on humanity."

Helen Greiner, Chairman and former President of iRobot:

"Getting reports back from areas where our military is engaged in combat saying that our product saved lives—those are my absolute proudest moments."

And so on and so on. Being in the presence of such leaders kept calling me to a higher place in myself, questioning who I was and what I represented through the choices I had made and those I had avoided. Do I have the courage to follow my own inner guidance system and live my life more purposefully? When I die will I feel used up, knowing that I gave fully to the world from a deep sense of purpose? The more I engage with these questions, the more my choices become clear and my actions pure.

A Leader's Inner Journey

I met Susanna Post about five years ago when the company she helped run as COO was being sold. After lengthy negotiations the buyout firm finally bought the company with the stipulation that the current CEO had to leave. Happy to get the money he felt he deserved, the founder took the offer and the new owners immediately replaced him with Susanna. She had never before been a CEO, and while she had great courage and determination, she also had many doubts about her ability to perform. Nonetheless, she took the position because she believed she could learn how to become great in her role as CEO and she believed deeply in the company and its potential. She then contacted me and asked if I would coach her and her company to realize this potential.

At the time the company had enjoyed more than 20 years of consistent growth. While signs of a sales plateau loomed, the market looked promising, and the new owners were confident that, with an infusion of cash, the company could expand beyond its successful past and position itself to go public.

Following an initial diagnosis of the organization's health, Susanna set three tasks for herself. First, she strengthened the leadership team by letting go of several vice-presidents and replacing them with stronger players. Second, she reduced the overall number of VPs. Up until then the executive team was too large, making it incapable of making quick decisions. Third, she began weeding out much of the corruption that plagued the sales force—a legacy left behind by the organization's founder. Along the way, she continued her commitment to growing and learning and to becoming as strong a leader as she could.

After three years of work with the team and letting go of well over half the sales management of the company, she and I assessed her progress. The biggest change she made was moving her company from basically a one-product platform to one with multiple lines of businesses, all stemming from the company's strong original brand. This was no small feat, as their original product enjoyed continued robust sales; extending the brand risked financial failure and spreading the company too thin. Undaunted, Susanna made a number of changes to grow new products and set the company up for future success.

Despite these improvements, there was much that was still to be accomplished, including lingering ethical problems in sales and a leadership team that continued to blame one another and undermine effective teamwork. At the same time, Susanna had grown a great deal and was confident enough to take another bold step forward from which there would be no turning back. That step was the culmination of our two years of working together, with much of that time focused on making tactical changes in her leadership approach and helping her to get a handle on her business as a whole.

As we considered her progress and looked to the future, it became clear that Susanna still didn't feel comfortable in herself. While she felt she was making sound business decisions that were paying off, the company wasn't yet what she wanted it to be. Most importantly, she felt she had failed in building a strong leadership team and that, while improvements in the integrity of sales people were evident, it was still unsatisfactory. We decided to go deeper.

The turning point came after a series of coaching sessions where the primary focus was to find her life purpose. During this process, both of us sensed that she was driven by a desire deeper than just running a strong business. She felt she was meant for something bigger and more fulfilling, but she couldn't put her finger on what that was. Over a period of a few months we set about finding the answer.

Every two weeks we spent time on the phone exploring her desires and her dreams—including those she remembered while sleeping; observing the patterns of her concerns; and ultimately trying to follow a path into her soul. Feeling like we were close to the finish line, we decided to spend an entire day together, and through a series of exercises designed to quiet her mind so she could listen to what stirred within, Susanna finally discovered her purpose. It revealed itself very simply. In fact, it wasn't far from what she had been telling herself all along but never completely "got." She wanted to transform the world of both her customers and her employees so that they would experience abundance, satisfaction, and well-being. From that moment on she was on a mission; the tree of purpose had rooted itself deep within her. No longer was the company just a place to work and to be helpful. The changes she began to make were immediate and made without hesitation. Her bearing became more regal and her sense of resolve became apparent to all. She began to relax into her role as CEO, claiming it fully for herself. In short, she felt she had finally arrived. She had discovered, as all great leaders do, that an organization's purpose is directly influenced by its leader's focus and certainty of direction—his or her inner compass.

Such clarity is difficult to come by, though you wouldn't know it by the marketing materials of many organizational consultants or the simplistic formulas found in many books. They try to convince you that corporate re–visioning can be achieved in "five-eight-ten easy steps," and hoist as examples various companies and leaders that demonstrate a degree of vision and success. "You, too, can be one of them," they exclaim. "All you need is this process!"

"It takes three days, you say?" asks the CEO. "We don't have that kind of time. Do you have a more efficient process?"

"Sure," says the consultant, who wants the business. "We can do that. We'll give you the express methodology." And so each party enters into a quick and dirty contract that will only skate the surface, hoping that the results will end up meaning something. But they rarely do, for a truly powerful vision is not arrived at so easily. There is no "express methodology."

For years I plied my trade as a "culture change" consultant offering various ways for organizations to reach their vision, and it's a hit-or-miss proposition at best. More often than not, the vision statements are artificial. Sure, we print banners and order mugs emblazoned with a slogan, but over time, business as usual resumes. And I wasn't the only one. Thousands of consultants had the same results. The fault lies in the misbegotten belief that one can *have* a vision. Vision is not something one *has*. It is something one *is*.

When they started their business in their garage, William Hewlett didn't turn to David Packard and say, "Gee, Dave, we ought to get us one of those vision statements. All the great companies have one." Nor did Tom Watson or Henry Ford or other great visionaries think in such a way. Their drive, passion, focus, and purpose came from a place that lay deep in the belly, burning like a furnace and centered in their soul's joy. They could do nothing else but give expression to it. That flame burned strong and golden not because they made it up but because they found what already existed and had the courage to live it.

I realize that all this talk of purpose has a tendency to cause people's eyes to glaze over. "Yeah, yeah, I know—people have to have a purpose," is a typical response. It strikes them as obvious or corny or beneath them in some way, as if the thought is an accusation that the lives they are living are rudderless. And so we hurry on to more respectable (and safer) considerations, those that make us less uncomfortable.

But when we feel most uncomfortable is precisely the time that we need to stop and follow that discomfort to the golden flame burning bright—but unrecognized—deep within. When we do, we will recognize five truths about the connections between strong leadership and an inner compass:

✓ *Remarkable leaders don't have a purpose; they are their purpose.*
Great leaders do not hold their purpose as an idea outside of themselves. They live it. They breathe it. It permeates all they do. It

is not something they need to be reminded of, nor is it something that needs to be expressed in words.

✓ *Every significant action of a remarkable leader is driven by their purpose.* They feel the tug of their purpose every day, in every moment. They don't take actions that are inconsistent with their purpose.

✓ *A great leader's vision is a tangible expression of a purpose directed toward a particular cause.* Remarkable leaders direct their purpose toward something of real value. The "vision thing" is the expression of their purpose in a form that helps others to see it and know it for themselves.

✓ *Visionary leaders declare their vision as a* fait accompli *and then start manifesting it.* When President Kennedy declared that we would send a man to the moon and back by the end of the 1960s, he had no rational basis for such a claim. In fact, the experts around him said that it was impossible. He persevered nonetheless and drew people to him who believed in the dream and were willing to create the needed technology where none existed. Such leaders believe that a vision is a "done deal" and then proceed to make it so.

✓ *Visionary leaders declare their vision publicly, and are willing to accept failure.* By declaring their vision publicly, they put a stake in the ground and accept responsibility for everything that happens next.

There is no better way to express this notion of purpose-centered leadership than in the words of Mary Taverna, president of Hospice of Marin in California. In reflecting what inspired her to play such an instrumental role in bringing the hospice movement to the U.S. in the 1970s, she told me, "You know, Keith, we're put on this earth for reasons unknown and we're given our gifts. How we apply those gifts is completely up to us."

✧

Remarkable leaders apply these gifts toward a higher purpose; such commitment gives meaning to their life and an enduring experience of satisfaction to their soul. From this powerful sense of purpose and clarity, they create and follow a map that guides them and gives shape to the daily choices they make. Our next chapter explores this territory more deeply.

KEY POINTS IN CHAPTER 3

- Remarkable leaders have a sense of calling—they are driven by a deep sense of purpose.

- It is from this sense of purpose that their clarity of vision, courage, determination and drive is derived.

- Leadership is a game of influence.

- Great leadership is about influencing others toward a larger and more profound aim that uplifts and adds meaningful value to the world.

- For remarkable leaders, purpose is not something one has; it is who one is.

CHAPTER 4

✧

A CLEAR MAP

The measure of a man's real character is what he
would do if he knew he never would be found out.
—*Lord Thomas Macaulay*

As I write this chapter, I reflect back on a decisive moment in my career. A couple of years ago, I faced the troubling awareness that my small consulting company had not yet become what I had envisioned it to be. It would be easy to just stand on my laurels—years of modest success had bred comfort—but I sensed that the company was poised at a precipice of new possibilities. Our "boutique" business model wasn't well designed to attract top consulting talent, which had kept us from growing, but I knew that we hadn't yet tapped our potential. So I faced an enormous challenge: change the model and make a more meaningful impact in the world or accept that we would always remain small. It was a major decision that I hesitated to make.

The hesitation was rooted in a fear of loss. If I pushed for growth in the direction I believe the firm needed to go, I might lose some of my current partners, which I did not want to happen—our camaraderie and mutual support had defined our culture. And yet my intuition kept telling me that we could be much greater than we were. Even more to the point, I knew that *I* had the potential to be much greater. The deeper question, then, was not so much about my company but about me. What was I willing to risk to play a much bigger game than I'd been playing?

An internal battle between fear and purpose had me in its grip. "Why upset the apple cart?" cautioned a conservative part of me. I had reached middle age and a life of comfort and consistency was attractive. And yet if I didn't tip that cart, how would I feel on my deathbed, knowing that I had turned away from my soul's desire to create the firm of my dreams, from a chance to become bigger than I was?

The choice was simple: Honor my purpose and grow as a human being, or give in to my fears and remain locked in unrealized potential. It is a choice that everyone faces many times in his or her life. The difference with great leaders is that they consistently choose to grow, in service to their soul's calling. And whether I made the same choice or not ultimately depended on how I responded to my own inner wisdom. My fear said "No," reflecting the truth about the number one criticism leveled by my partners about my own leadership skills: that I often resisted expressing what I wanted. They loved my willingness to facilitate and honor everyone's views in the spirit of collaboration, but they missed a certain resolve that they believed was there, lurking beneath the surface of my accommodating demeanor.

I've always had a strong capacity to express myself and do so in other contexts, but in my own firm, that authoritative voice was lacking. Looking at my hesitation in archetypal terms, I had not embraced the King in me, though I sat on the throne as founder and leader. Ironically, I have counseled many leaders to step up into their own power and carry the scepter that is rightfully theirs, and I had certainly found my own voice as a consultant. But I had fallen prey to one of the taboos in "new age" leadership: the stigma of being an authoritative leader.

The Taboo of Authoritative Leadership

Nowhere is there more confusion, misconception, or misapplication in the world of leadership than around the concept of "authority." Up until the mid-nineteenth century, being an authoritative leader was seen as an asset, a sought-after quality associated with captains of sea vessels, military leaders, and successful industrialists. At the time, authoritative leadership had to do with the ability and willingness to stand for something meaningful, to step away from the herd and offer a clear and compelling vision, to make the tough decisions and then stay the course with courage and determination. In years past, such abilities were considered honorable and even crucial. But the influence of a new model of leadership called "participative management" slowly eroded the legitimacy of the role of the authoritative leader.

> *Nowhere is there more confusion, misconception, or misapplication in the world of leadership than around the concept of "authority."*

This process of erosion started in the 1960s and continued through the 1980s as studies began to demonstrate that leaders who included others in decision making and in shaping their work culture typically produced higher levels of commitment, ownership, teamwork, and flexibility among their employees—crucial capacities in a fast-changing world. Companies that cultivated this capacity in their leaders were more likely to be profitable in the long run, boasting lower turnover rates and higher staff satisfaction.[1] At the same time, an impressive body of research on the impacts of dictatorial leadership styles also started accumulating. It showed, not surprisingly, that such rigid approaches could cause problems in the workplace, such as concentrations of power and the creation of a fear-driven work culture.

The cumulative effect of this research and the leadership training efforts associated with it has been to encourage an entire generation of leaders to adopt some of the gentler skills of leadership. They have been trained, for example, to *facilitate* decision making, to *coach* their employees, and to demonstrate true *caring* for others. In the span of roughly 30 years, the preeminence of authoritative leadership has given way to participative leadership and, yes, something important has been gained. I recognize the value of participatory leadership when applied judicially, as did all of the leaders I interviewed. Andrea Youngdahl, head of human services for the city of Oakland, said, "I much prefer to work *with* staff rather than talk down to them." Chris Chavez, CEO of Advanced Neuromodulation Systems, told me, "I like leaders to be conductors—they ultimately work through people." CEO of Atlas Container, Paul Centenari, and his brother have created an extraordinary organization defined by extreme democracy. At Atlas, everyone gets to vote on all key decisions that affect him or her directly and that affect the organization as a whole.

At the same time that something has been gained, something has also been lost. Sadly, the word "authority" in the business lexicon has become weighted down with derogatory baggage. Now when we think of authority, we too often imagine someone who hoards control over others in a structure of hierarchy and zealous rule-making or a person with significant knowledge—an "expert" on a particular subject—whose opinion can't be challenged. We are reminded by countless bumper stickers to "question authority" as if any kind of leadership is cause for suspicion.

However, our emotional reactions to such narrow definitions of the concept of authority miss a deeper point: The root word in authority is "author." At its most meaningful level, someone with authority is the author of themselves, the author of their own lives. They believe in their capabilities and express themselves without hesitation. Their sense of authority comes not from a belief in their superiority over others but from an experience of inner clarity and strength. Such is the essence of the sense of "gravitas" I spoke of in Chapter 2. As I observe the depth to which partic-ipative leadership has taken root, I am not so much troubled by how many leaders practice authoritative leadership; I am troubled by how few practice it well.

Thankfully, there are models to the contrary. As I listened to the remarkable leaders I met, I found that each of their voices was compelling and clear—authoritative in the deeper meaning of the term—and imbued with their own inner conviction, often quietly expressed. Because they were deeply grounded in who they were, they didn't feel a need to shout. Yet they drew me in and kept my attention. And because they were clear about who they were and what they valued, they found it easy to allow others to express themselves.

Take a moment and reflect on your own life. Do you have a clear sense of what you want to accomplish in your company? What do you want others to accomplish? What is your image of how people best work together? What troubles you about your organization? And the big question: To what extent have you made your vision, your values, and your desires known? If you've taken unequivocal stands in front of others, then your authoritative voice has been established. If not, then you are likely holding back your power from others and, more importantly, from yourself. Archimedes, the Greek mathematician and philosopher, is famous for saying: "Give me a fulcrum and a place to stand, and I will change the world." I believe that a place to stand has to do with holding a point of view and firmly expressing it. If one does this at the proper time and place (the fulcrum), one *can* change the world.

> *I am not so much troubled by how many leaders practice authoritative leadership; I am troubled by how few practice it well.*

The authoritative voice of remarkable leaders draws from all three primary conditions that are the focus of this book: a clear compass, a powerful inner anchor, and a solid sense of self. It is most evident in the ability of these leaders to communicate a map for success—not so much as a pithy vision or a compelling destination (often considered the sine qua non of great leadership) but as a fully fleshed-out direction with clear signposts of success.

These powerful maps can be both personal and organizational. Personal maps are guides for how to conduct yourself while honoring your personal purpose. Organizational maps represent a clear philosophy for how an organization will achieve success.

> *Personal maps are guides for how*
> *to conduct yourself while*
> *honoring your personal purpose.*

A Personal Map for Leadership Success

Many years ago I applied for a managerial position at a large consulting and training company. I got the job and reported to the man who interviewed me, Jac Cuney, vice-president of the West Coast region. During my interview, I found Jac to be wonderfully clear about his beliefs and what he was doing in the organization he led. I asked him how he had achieved such clarity.

"I wasn't always this clear," he replied. "In fact, as a manager I suffered for a long time from not being certain about who I was and where I was going. Then I reflected long and hard about what I stood for. In this process, I began to develop my own set of rules for how to be the best leader I could be. Here, let me show you." Jac pulled out a leather organizer and opened it to the first page. "Here are my principles for leadership. I developed them a long time ago, and they've served me well. Every morning, at the beginning of the day, I review them to remind me what to do."

I was surprised to see some very simple principles: *Be honest, no matter what. Listen with an open heart. Play win-win. Always know your priorities.* One item on the list was especially intriguing: *Remember that everything is about sales.*

"What does that mean?" I asked.

"It means that everything we do in this organization affects our ability to sell," he responded in the same calm yet firm voice that I heard so often in my meetings with remarkable leaders—one of self-assurance without a hint of arrogance. "If we don't produce a good product, it impairs sales. If we don't respond well to our customers, it impairs sales. Every function, no matter what, has an indirect or direct impact on sales. I want to remember this, and I want all of the people in the organization to get it—

and to get that what they do matters. When people get this principle, everyone pulls their oars in the same direction." (This particular principle has stayed with me—I often share it with clients as a way to help them get more aligned as a company.)

What impressed me about the list was how useful it was to Jac; it was literally his map. Later in our meeting, Jac said to me, "Whenever I feel off as a leader, I go back to the list and inevitably discover that I have violated one or more of my principles. It guides me back on track." The other thing that impressed me during the time I worked for and with him is that I cannot remember Jac ever deviating from that map. He lived those principles impeccably and, as a result, he earned my utmost respect and the respect of those who worked with him.

Having an internal map and using it as a guide seems deceptively simple on the surface, but there is complexity below. You see, we're all made up of many parts inside ourselves. There's a part that likes to be taken care of, for example, and another one that likes to give. We have a tender inner child and a raging control freak, a bully and a deeply sensitive side that wouldn't hurt a fly. There's the self-critical parent, the soulful lover, and many others. In many ancient traditions, from Greek tragedies to Hindu storytelling, these internal parts were often expressed in archetypal terms. Nearly all of our ancient myths, for example, were stories not of the outer world but expressions of the rich landscape of our inner world and the challenges associated with its mastery. Among the "Ten Commandments for Reading Myths" presented by the contemporary mythologist Joseph Campbell in his book *Myths to Live By* was this: "Read myths in the first person plural: the gods and goddesses of ancient mythology still live within you."

Mastery over the dynamics of our many "selves" has to do with the capacity to know those inner parts and wisely choose which one to express moment by moment. People who know themselves in this way and who have developed a healthy and aware ego have a much greater capacity for wise leadership and life success. Stated another way, remarkable leadership has to do with bringing out the best in ourselves. Being more self-aware, more *conscious*, is the key. Acting on and reinforcing one's highest mature expression differentiates great leaders from others. That list was helpful to Jac in many ways, the most important being that it reminded him to bring his best self—his best parts—forward in service to great leadership.

Most of the leaders I met on my journey had a personal philosophy to guide their choices—a belief system about what works and what doesn't and an abiding trust in that system. This philosophy enabled them to make decisions quickly and easily because it gave them a sense of sureness—precious commodities in the sea of uncertainty in which we all swim.

Betsy Bernard, former president of AT&T and, at the time, voted by *Fortune* magazine as one of the country's most powerful female business leaders, has been guided by her "golden rules of leadership" for many years. She first expressed them publicly at a conference for women, and they were so well received that she's been sharing them at talks ever since.[2]

* **Golden Rule No. 1:** Everyone's time is valuable. Everyone's. The CEO. The newest entry level. Everyone.

* **Golden Rule No. 2:** No temper tantrums. You should never have to say "no temper tantrums" to anyone after pre-school.

* **Golden Rule No. 3:** Get to the bloody point!

* **Golden Rule No. 4:** Be candid.

* **Golden Rule No. 5:** Just say "thank you." And mean it.

* **Golden Rule No. 6:** Integrity is everything. I don't want to work with you if you don't have it.

* **Golden Rule No. 7:** "If you don't know, who does?" In other words, vision.

Well before our time, great leaders similarly developed maps for themselves. George Washington developed such a map when he was 16 years old and called it, "Rules of Civility and Decent Behaviour in Company and Conversation." Those rules are generally regarded by historians as having been crucial in influencing the development of his character. They included guidelines for behavior in social company, appropriate actions in formal situations, and general courtesies such as "Superfluous Complements and all Affectation of Ceremonie are to be avoided, yet where due they are not to be Neglected"; "Think before you Speak"; and "Rinse not your Mouth in the Presence of Others." In using these rules as a map for his own conduct, Washington eventually became known as a man whose actions and character were beyond reproach.

> *Most of the leaders I met on my journey have a belief system about what works and what doesn't and an abiding trust in that system.*

As a young man Ben Franklin also had a map for himself. Dissatisfied with the religious ethics of churches, he set out to develop a moral character in his own way. To do this he created a list of virtues and then developed a rigorous self-reflection practice that consisted of practicing one virtue each day. Each night he noted whether he had succeeded or failed in the performance of that particular virtue. Franklin's list consisted of temperance, silence, order, resolution, frugality, industry, sincerity, justice, moderation, cleanliness, tranquility, chastity, and humility. He described each one so that his guidance was explicit and clear: *Temperance—Eat not to dullness, drink not to elevation; Order—Let all your things have their places, let each part of your business have its time; Moderation—Avoid extremes, forbear resenting injuries, so much as you think they deserve; Tranquility—Be not disturbed at trifles or at accidents common or unavoidable; Humility—Imitate Jesus and Socrates.* Once he went through the list, he cycled through it again, and over time this practice helped him mature into a man whom many came to admire and respect.

Interestingly, when I think about Washington and Franklin and many other great leaders of history, I think of their character more than anything else. The word "character" itself captures much of this spirit. It derives its meaning from the Greek word *kharakter*, which literally means, "engraved mark." People with strong character are known for a defining quality. They live consistently with a map that is engraved in their psyche so much so that it does not matter what others see, it only matters what a person of character sees in him or herself.

We all have personal maps that are guiding us, yet few of us know what they are, not having spent the time to get to know them. In the words of the popular 19th-century columnist George Matthew Adams,

> *Every one of us, unconsciously, works out a personal philosophy of life, by which we are guided, inspired, and corrected, as time goes on. It is this philosophy by which we measure out our days, and by which we advertise to all about us the man, or woman that we are. It takes but a brief time to scent the life philosophy of anyone. It is defined in the conversation, in the look of the eye, and in the general mien of the person. It has no hiding place. It's like the perfume of the flower — unseen, but known almost instantly.*

I believe, then, that one of the real differences between great and mediocre leaders is the extent to which they are conscious of their inner beliefs. Indeed, most of the leaders I spoke to could thoughtfully and clearly express their inner map for success. At the same time, some were guided more by their intuition. Mimi Silbert of the Delancey Street Foundation, for example, didn't have a defined personal leadership map. Instead, she searches her heart for guidance, trusting her inner knowing of what to do, and this has yet to fail her.

An Organizational Map for Success

One of my colleagues often begins her work with clients by asking, "What's the big idea?" This question requires that they think deeply and clearly about the focus point around which all other activities and decisions revolve. Remarkable leaders know what their big idea is. It is embedded in their map, guiding their organizational world toward specific goals.

Helen Greiner knows what her big idea is, and her entire company is organized around it. Helen is the co-founder and former Chairman and President of iRobot, the company known for the Roomba—a state-of-the-art vacuum cleaner that vacuums floors robotically. The country has much to thank Helen and her company for, because it also builds robots that are designed to disable landmines for military purposes and bombs for police operations.

During the interview, her presence was quiet and wonderfully unassuming. She, like so many others I met, had a kind of "Aw, shucks" way about her, as if to say, "I'm not so great. I'm just doing what I love and doing the best I can to contribute." But humility doesn't mean that she isn't crystal clear about her philosophy of leadership. She was. It had to do with giving talented people the right tools for expressing their brilliance and then giving them room to grow. Said Helen:

> We're just so motivated here, personally motivated. Our aim is to build cool stuff and answer customers' needs. If you set people in the right direction, it's amazing what comes out. Getting small teams together that are passionate about a certain subject is the key. Powerful ideas don't usually come from the top down but from the bottom up. This belief freed our people to do everything from changing the way the military operates to getting a top-selling consumer product on the market. It's about unleashing people's potential. We've proven this model of leadership several times, and I feel very strongly about it. We tried it the other way, you know, where I say, okay, do this, this, and this. That approach is not as powerful as when someone comes up with his or her own idea and then is given the chance to hit it out of the park.

Bannus Hudson, profiled in Chapter Two, had a particularly impressive map for the company he led. Bannus arrived at BevMo in 1997 as the new CEO, and after spending a few weeks learning about the company, he knew that he was facing a turnaround situation. The regional company sold popular wines, soft drinks, and accessories at a number of urban locations in California but was hurting financially. Having guided a successful transformation at LensCrafters, the now famous eyeglass retailer, Bannus quickly determined that BevMo needed a guiding vision and a clear and focused brand image, imperative in the highly competitive world of retail sales. "Anything I do today, somebody can duplicate tomorrow," he told me. "Our name trademark—that's about the only protection we have." He went on to explain that a trademark is much more than a visual image or a tagline; it's an enduring impression of what a company represents and stands for, and it is such an image that BevMo needed.

Bannus described the fleshed-out features of the map that had guided his organization for years, one that he knew intimately and completely.

> *Our differentiator had to be the person in the store dealing with the customer. It's about service, about wanting to take care of the customer. All this other stuff, how the store is laid out, the merchandise, the prices, the advertising and the expectations, all support that magic. You're going to have to drive by three grocery stores and the corner liquor store just to get to ours, so we have to do something to make you want to drive past those stores. It's partly value but really it's that green shirt (the color each employee wears) who is taking care of you that causes you to visit our store.*

Bannus spoke quietly but with enormous authority in a matter-of-fact tone. He didn't need to raise his voice because his inner authority spoke volumes.

Everything kind of flows from the clear map I provided for the company. Branding and strategic marketing is what they lacked the most, so that's what I provided: creating an image that BevMo is more than a big box with a bunch of stuff in it, and then figuring out how to convey that message to potential customers. Now the customer understands from experience that at BevMo they get a great selection with good value along with knowledgeable people who will make their visit fun. Entertaining, educational, and knowledgeable, but primarily fun. People now want to shop at BevMo!

I can easily imagine Bannus standing in front of a group of store managers, drilling into them this central notion of customer experience, then explaining how it gets implemented through an organizational map for getting from where you are to where you want to be. Like most good organizational maps, his reflected a theory or philosophy of management and leadership that helped others to focus more clearly on the goals. Note the simplicity and clarity of his message:

Focus comes out of the process. It's being sure that you're doing a couple of things really well as opposed to a lot of things pretty well. People kid me about this, but I believe you have three reasons for doing anything—not two, not four, but three. There's some magic to me in the number three because two isn't enough and four is too many. We thus spend a lot of time defining what our three focus areas are for each year, a process we're in right now. We start by reviewing wins, what have we done that has worked. What are we doing really well that will make a difference in the organization? And if we failed at something, what did we learn? From all this we decide on the three primary areas and then the planning comes.

*   It is no surprise, then, that there is a strong relationship between a clear map and organizational success. Recent research on the factors that stimulate organic growth in business reinforces the importance of a simple strategic map to guide an organization—to help ensure everyone is rowing in the same direction.[3]

Clear and Open

Whether a map is personal, organizational, or both, two important features make them powerful—when the leaders holding them are clear and open. In other words, while remarkable leaders are able to express their beliefs without hesitation, they are also receptive to the views of others. While the vision, values, and fundamental strategy for their organizations provide clear direction and allow for powerfully aligned efforts, the how of getting there—what people do and how they work together—is open to dialogue and exploration. This requires that the leader be equally facile in holding on and letting go, both anchored in a personal vision and participating in the route to achieve it. Someone once told me that the definition of a leader is "Someone willing to go it alone....and to never going it alone." This phrase says something crucial about the essence of great leadership—the need to stand on one's own two feet while artfully enlisting the energy and ideas of others.

Remarkable leadership, then, is not a compromise between the authoritative and the participative as the following diagram might imply:

Figure 4-1: Imagined Sweet Spot

Instead it requires the capacity to meld the two into one—to be simultaneously authoritative and participative.

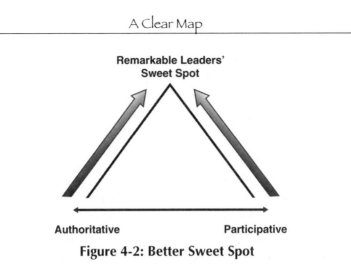

Figure 4-2: Better Sweet Spot

Being open to others' views comes from being clear and comfortable about one's own perspective—from self-confidence and inner strength—*and* from an understanding that collaboration unleashes the power of the collective.

The Path toward Inner Authority

Craig has been a salesperson all his adult life. He is street savvy and intelligent with a healthy dose of compassion that makes him genuinely eager to help others. As a result, he chose to work in the healthcare field early in his career. He has many of the typical behavioral characteristics one finds among career salespeople—friendly, outgoing, and charming—but he also prides himself on wanting to do the right thing for his clients and the company he represents, while making a good living for his family.

Craig has worked primarily for large companies, moving naturally up the career ladder. Recently he landed a position as head of sales for a company of 500 people, responsible for setting the strategy and leading a team of 55 people toward achieving increasingly challenging sales targets. Hoping to reach his stride as a leader, he instead hit a wall.

The wall was the CEO who, unlike most of the leaders Craig had worked for, was a man of impeccable integrity. When Craig arrived, the CEO was successfully building a company of substance, size, and reputation, and a culture based on a clear and nonnegotiable set of values.

Craig saw himself as a man of integrity, but quickly found that he was a bit slippery on the edges. For example, it was perfectly acceptable in other companies he had worked for to pick up a dinner tab and label the expense a customer call, even when that might not be the case. It was also acceptable to treat oneself to a high-quality hotel room and an expensive meal when working in the field. After all, thought Craig along with many of his former sales colleagues, we work hard and deserve it. In a big company that is doing well, many of these practices are hidden and acceptable, and Craig fell right in with the crowd.

In his new company, however, both his peers and the CEO considered such practices to be self-serving and lacking in integrity. Why try to "get something" from a company that relied for its success on everyone pulling together and giving generously to each other and its customers? It was simply the wrong spirit, and Craig's integrity quickly came under suspicion. Moreover, Craig talked too much, acting like he was smarter than his peers and knew more about the industry than they did. His prima donna profile didn't fit the corporate culture, and his future in the company looked increasingly uncertain.

When I met Craig, he desperately wanted to turn the situation around. He respected the company, the CEO, and his peers, and knew that his behavior was problematic. In meeting with him for a few sessions, it became clear that not only was he used to behaving in ways that some companies considered common practice, but that Craig had never developed an internal map for himself. The companies he had worked for all had strong cultures and long histories. He had moved up the ranks by getting along, doing a good job, and following the rules already set by others before him. For all his working life he'd been the "hale fellow well met," easy with people and very forgiving. He was the quintessential company man, without a map to call his own.

I began by asking him to articulate a set of goals for himself. Among the most important were that he would act with honesty and integrity at work and with me, and that he would take full responsibility for his actions and their consequences. If ever he made a mistake or failed to produce the outcome he wanted, he would own up to his contribution instead of blaming others, which he admitted was one of his tendencies. Early on I noticed that when I asked him what he wanted to do about a difficult situation at work, he would often look to me for answers or end up asking the CEO. This pattern of dependency confirmed for me that Craig had never developed an inner authority to guide him in making his own decisions.

The act of building one's inner authority is no small feat. It requires a huge amount of courage to face oneself in the mirror, tell the truth, and forge ahead into unknown territory without the comfort of doing that which you have always done or that which others have done before you. Thankfully, Craig had that courage, and he knew somewhere deep inside that for him to grow, to become the leader he wanted to become and the kind admired by others, this was a crucial step to take.

After establishing his goals, Craig next got clear about his core values and what he stood for—not because the CEO or the company said so but because he said so. This process took time as Craig searched his heart and looked back on his experiences to find the principles that had always been there but that he hadn't always followed. It was a difficult journey as he recalled the many times he hadn't acted from integrity.

The next step, the longest and perhaps the most challenging, was actually developing his inner map. He wrestled with such questions as "What do I believe in?", "Who am I in this situation?", and "What is unacceptable to me?" Little by little, always starting with the question, "If it were solely up to me, what would I do?" Craig began to forge his internal guidance system for leading. This didn't mean that it was *always* up to Craig to make a final decision or that others couldn't be involved, for it was easy for Craig to include others in the process. It was about Craig making sure that he included himself in the decision-making process instead of always deferring to an outside authority.

The first step for Craig in applying what he was learning was to develop, along with his team, the goals for the sales division and the key processes and practices they would use to achieve those goals. Along the way, it was Craig's job not only to contribute to these goals but also to be clear about his own personal boundaries—taking stands, pushing back, and putting a stake in the ground when needed. Over a span of several months, his map was developed, his integrity solidified, and his leadership skills began to mature and yield results.

It Cannot Be Copied

Certainty and self-confidence about one's choices and actions come from a clear internal map that is uniquely one's own. It cannot be made up. It's not a philosophy borne from watching others and then choosing what one likes.

A colleague articulated for me what I have been sensing for a long time: Great leaders ultimately and courageously go beyond imitation to find their own mature expression—their leadership signature, if you will—that comes from the deepest part of themselves. We'll explore this more in Chapter 11.

Back at my own company, the decision of whether to settle for the status quo or take the big risk toward change and growth turned out to be more difficult *and* simpler than I had imagined. The difficult part was in realizing that even when I knew I was my own worst enemy, afraid to take a stand, I still dragged my heels, weighing various options for months. The simple part was what happened when I finally made the decision to honor my purpose and vision.

Facing my dubious partners at a seminal company meeting, I declared, "No longer am I content to play the small game we've been playing. We have not fulfilled our original vision, and I'm growing restless. It is time for us to grow, and I will not rest until we become who I believe we are destined to be as a company." I then laid out my plan—the map as well as the destination—and asked them if they were with me. Their answer confirmed that the problem had been me all along. "What took you so long?" they asked.

◈

I believe that the most crucial mindset for leadership in this day and age is that we create the future. This notion is a fundamentally new paradigm. It is no longer possible to assume the future by extrapolating from the past. We must create it. Such is the essence of a great leader's powerful vision and it comes from a deeper place than most leaders dwell—a deep inner compass. In effect both a clear sense of purpose and a clear map form the two-part fixtures of that powerful inner compass— the source from which a leader is able to imagine, articulate and ultimately navigate the future.

Having now explored the importance of an inner compass and what that entails, we now turn to the second force that gives rise to great leadership—being anchored in one's values. This force has two characteristics: applying a set of principles that lives deep within, and cultivating a sense of care that guides one's life.

KEY POINTS IN CHAPTER 4

- Remarkable leaders have a clear sense of what they want to create. Their sense of outer authority comes from a sense of inner authority.

- Authoritative leadership and autocratic leadership are not at all the same. The former inspires. The latter controls.

- Great leaders have a personal map to guide them. They know when they are on track and when they are off.

- Their organizational map is derived from their personal map.

- Great leaders are both clear and open.

CHAPTER 5

---- ✧ ----

THE ANCHOR OF VALUES

This above all: to thine own self be true,
And it must follow, as the night the day,
Thou canst not then be false to any man.
Farewell; my blessing season this in thee!
—William Shakespeare

I could hear myself droning on and on, and I didn't feel settled in my body. I was in a meeting with a prospective new client to explore whether or not he wanted to work with me. The president had brought me in on the pretense that the CEO would be inspired enough by what I had to say to hire me as a consultant. What the president apparently told him, casually and in so many words, was, "I want you to meet this guy Keith. He seems to have something worth listening to." What the president did not say to me was, "I'm having a lot of difficulty working with my CEO, and I want you to help him see what a problem he is for me and the company as a whole." He was, in short, avoiding a confrontation with his CEO by using me in the guise of this meeting to do it for him—a clear case of manipulation. And though this was a dawning suspicion, I wanted the work and decided to go with the flow.

The meeting did not go well. The conversation between us felt stilted, the president's unspoken agenda pulling at me like an undertow. I listened carefully to the CEO and offered my perspective, but it all felt pushy, like a sales pitch. The words were right; the feeling was not. I had not dropped down into my deepest truth, which wanted to say, "Let's stop pretending and get down to the reason I was asked to be here." And so my words droned on but didn't land.

How many times had I felt such a feeling, knowing something was off but avoiding the message while trying to dazzle someone with slick words? This is not great leadership and certainly not great consulting, and it showed to this perceptive CEO. Nothing clicked, for I wasn't listening and speaking from my heart. I didn't feel right in my body; I had a physical experience of fragmentation, and my body always tells the truth. And now it was telling me, "You're out of integrity."

An Inner Anchor

While an inner compass has to do with knowing one's purpose and having an internal map as a guide, an inner anchor is different. It has to do with being crystal clear about your values. Almost all the leaders I met had such an anchor. With unshakeable clarity they talked with ease about the everyday values that counted for them, such as honesty, trust, and reliability. I have often heard such words voiced by other leaders, but they didn't ring true.

In the popular musical comedy, *Damn Yankees*, a distinguished gentleman named Mr. Applegate offers Joe Boyd, an aging, lifelong fan of the Washington Senators baseball team, a proposition: to become young again and lead the Senators, who could never seem to defeat the powerful New York Yankees, to the pennant. In exchange Joe will have to sell his soul and can never return to his family. After great angst, he signs on the dotted line. Like the long-suffering fan Joe Boyd, many of us sell our soul to our own version of the devil, seduced by the chance for fame, fortune, or glory. Except, that is, for the leaders I met on my journey. Perhaps they succumbed back in their youth, but now, for many of them, no amount of money is large enough to compromise their deepest sense of who they are and what they believe in. Just as impressive is how the immovable force of their connection to their values shows up not as pride or a feeling of being special but as something quite ordinary. "Yes, of course, I'm probably considered an honest person, but let's talk about something else..."

And they did. Exuding a combination of calm and fierce resolve, they shared wonderful stories of their own inner knowing at work. Those stories often included the hard choices they had to make, but they always reflected a walk that matched their talk. I am reminded of Jerry Jampolsky, the highly successful psychiatrist who decided to listen to his heart and stop charging for his services. He almost went broke, but his guiding value of generosity left him no other choice—then led to unexpected riches.

> *Almost all the leaders I met talked with ease about the everyday values that counted for them.*

I hesitate to write about values, for so much has been written already. And yet I cannot deny that values do matter, and they matter a lot. The research demonstrates that all great leaders are guided by an inner set of values—whether or not they express them in words. In his best-selling book *True North*,[1] former Medtronic CEO Bill George interviewed 125 outstanding leaders and came to the same conclusion: The best leaders are anchored in values. In George's words, they know where "true north" is, and their unwavering resolve to march in that direction is truly inspirational. In fact what impressed me most about the leaders I met is that almost all of them had faced powerful choices in their life where they gave up something important in order to honor their core values. Scott Johnson gave up a lucrative consulting career to follow his heart and start the Myelin Repair Foundation. Betsy Bernard walked away from her role as president of AT&T because her inner guidance system told her that something felt wrong about some of the expectations she faced. Paul Centenari, CEO of Atlas Container, put his company, his career, and all of his wealth at risk to follow his heart and create a company based on an out-of-the-box and untested version of organizational democracy. Charles Garcia may have given up the potential for a successful career in politics for standing up for what he believed in. His story is especially compelling.

In 1997, with $800,000 in personal funds and seed money from family and friends, Garcia founded the Sterling Financial Investment Group (SFIG). By 2001 SFIG claimed a worldwide network of more than 400 independent agents working out of more than 50 offices in the United States and eight offices worldwide including Panama, Spain, Chile, Greece, and England. As a result, Garcia was named by *Hispanic Magazine* as one of the "100 most influential Hispanics in the United States."

Along with his formidable business achievements, Charles is actively involved in politics, and he shared a story that aptly captures the true mark of what it means to be anchored in one's values. During the George W. Bush administration, he was invited to participate in a committee responsible for addressing the needs of Hispanics in U.S. education policy. The Bush administration, with its reputation for "groupthink," had established some important education policy guidelines, which many of the President's supporters felt obligated to agree with and reinforce. Charles, however, didn't agree with this direction, and was told by many of his political colleagues that if he didn't go along with it he would potentially face political suicide.

Charles's integrity meant more to him than anything else, and so with a pounding heart and an acute awareness that his potential political career was at stake, he took his perspective directly to the President. Those who had warned Charles not to contradict their views weren't happy with this decision and threatened him by suggesting he would be ruined in politics. Charles was not dissuaded. Unwilling to compromise what he believed in, he met with Bush and, to the President's credit, Bush expressed appreciation for Charles' perspective and thanked him for his candor. Many of his colleagues declared that his political career was severely compromised. That may have been true, but to this day Charles stands by his decision.

Like Garcia, John Wooden, the Hall of Fame UCLA basketball coach who presided over a dynasty unparalleled in the annals of modern college sports, was a shining example of someone who was immovable about his values. One of them addressed how players conducted themselves in public. For example, Wooden wanted his athletes to dress well, not because he was stuffy but because he wanted them to carry themselves with pride and dignity. Bill Walton, who turned out to be the finest college player of his generation, decided to test Wooden by demanding to keep his beard and to dress however he wanted. Bill was a bright, fiercely independent student with an engaging personality and inquisitive mind who was obviously willing to challenge authority. When faced with Walton's insistence to "do his own thing," Wooden responded, "We're going to miss you, Bill." Walton chose to live by Wooden's expectations, and the rest is history: Walton became the central force during UCLA's dominance in the early 70s. In refusing to compromise on his values, Wooden was willing to lose his star performer and put the UCLA program at significant risk.

What was it about Wooden's values that made him such a great leader? Was it the fact that he cared about those values? Hardly. Everyone has values, including those who have risen to similar levels of leadership in NCAA Division I basketball. In fact without a clear set of values you wouldn't stand a chance of achieving such a position. So then was it the content of Wooden's values? I doubt that as well, insofar as many coaches, particularly of his generation, care about dignity and respect, and there are plenty of mediocre leaders with those very same values. I believe the reason Wooden stood out was the immovability of his values. They reflected the deepest sense of who he was and weren't negotiable. As a result, there was no alternative for Wooden but to live them.

In being anchored to their core values, Wooden and other great leaders can be counted on to be trustworthy. You may not necessarily agree with their values, but you can trust that they will act consistently and impeccably. And in my estimation, it's that very same trust that acts like glue holding an organization together. Some might say that it was foolish for Wooden to risk success over such a small thing as a dress code. I would say the opposite: It was the principle underneath the code and the fact that he never wavered from it that was the source of Wooden's success. It fueled Wooden's golden flame, a flame that continues to cast a powerful light in spite of his having retired more than 30 years ago.

Embracing Values

I've had the pleasure of both witnessing and guiding powerful instances of what it means to live one's values. In one example I was working with a company and its leadership to help them become a significant force in their industry. When I first arrived, the company's revenues had been growing steadily but profits were falling. Soon the company started hemorrhaging money, a fact that growing revenues and a revolving door of CFOs had masked. After careful examination we discovered a huge fissure in their business model, and after months of losses, Arnold, the CEO, faced a difficult truth: The company had to lay people off.

After many conversations among the leadership about the criteria of the layoff and how they wanted to orchestrate it, they declared that the most important factor in determining who would stay was the degree to which an employee embraced the company's values. The most important of these were self-initiative and self-responsibility. The leadership team looked at each function one at a time and rated each employee based purely on those company values. Those at the lower end of the rating scale would be laid off regardless of their performance. They then constructed a communication strategy wherein each function leader would sit down with the group of people to be laid off and announce the decision. A seminal moment occurred when the head of customer service realized that two of his best friends would have to be let go. When someone suggested that because of these relationships he should pass the responsibility of communicating this news to someone else on the leadership team, he said, "No, I'm the one to tell them. It's my decision and I need to stand by it."

And so with a leap of faith that self-initiative and self-responsibility would be among the company's defining values going forward, the leaders began the process. Arnold, in one of the most beautiful acts of courage and grace that I have seen, faced the entire staff and announced, to the surprise of many, that they were about to commence a layoff. He explained that the primary reason was that he had taken his eye off the ball. For well over a year, he explained, he and his leadership team had been making decisions without clear gauges of profitability—like flying a plane without an altimeter—and that rather than confront the issue head-on with his accounting team, he kept putting his attention to other matters. He admitted that this was ultimately his responsibility, apologized profusely, and promised that it would never happen again. He then laid out the criteria for who was to be laid off. This left employees squirming in their seats, understandably uncomfortable with not knowing where they stood. That day, meetings took place throughout the company where everyone was informed of their fate. Nearly one-third of the staff was let go, even top performers.

The company's leadership feared that a massive exodus would follow, but the opposite occurred. While those who left were surprised and sometimes angry, those who remained were grateful, not just because they were spared the axe but also because the company took a stand for its values and Arnold took full ownership of the decision and the cause of the problems. He didn't duck his responsibility as they had seen so many other leaders do, blaming the accountants, the economy, or industry conditions, which breeds mistrust and low confidence. By taking full responsibility, Arnold re-energized the company's mission and the staff's loyalty.

Almost immediately the tone of the workplace changed. As they got a handle on their financial condition, the company began to perform at a very high level. Within four months it was performing even better than it had just before the layoff—with a third of its labor force missing!

Judith Rogala has made a lifetime of leading, and her perspective on leadership explains why the actions of "Arnold" and other great leaders (including herself) make sense. Among many other accomplishments, she was the only female on the executive team at Fed Ex in her role of running operations, and has since been a leader in many organizations, including Flagship Express, Office Depot and Le Petite Academy. When asked why so few leaders truly lead well, she told me,

> My definition of great leadership is knowing who you are, what you believe, and what your core values are, and then being true to those values. I have a saying: 'You can't

trust others until you trust yourself.' During an interview process, one V.P. came up to me and said, 'When you told me no politics here, I've got to tell you I didn't believe it. I believe it now.' And that political thing, however it comes about, is a real killer in an organization. People like to cover it over with something like, 'Oh, I've got a great team.' But many of those people within the team are not feeling satisfied because they have compromised their values. Some CEOs have unwittingly compromised his or her values as well. They're not being true to themselves. They're not authentic.

Judith's words rang true to me, and were echoed by all of the leaders I met. If a leader is unwilling to do whatever it takes to put values first, then those values aren't core. They are simply a means to an end and therefore lack potency.

The Road Less Traveled

In my career I've tried to be impeccably honest. In fact, I believe that many people have seen me as one of the more honest people they know. And perhaps I am, but there is much they couldn't see—the mini-lies or distortions of the truth to keep a client, spare someone's feelings, or impress a new acquaintance. In those moments when I knew I wasn't telling the truth, my body would slump in the knowing.

And so a few years ago I made a decision to never knowingly tell a lie or distort the truth no matter the consequences. The story told at the beginning of this chapter was a rare example to the contrary, and it was only after the meeting that I recognized I was out of integrity. This commitment to 100% integrity has been a hard one because I have had to take more risks and to face my greatest fears. At the same time, it has been quite liberating. When I act with integrity, I walk through an invisible threshold, standing tall in my authenticity.

It is this same erect stance that I saw in each of the leaders I met. Each walked tall in their values. One of the most inspiring meetings I had in this regard was with Ginger Graham, who resonated with inner strength and humility. When I met Ginger, she was the CEO of Amylin, a biopharmaceutical company that specializes in researching therapies for people with diabetes. When Ginger first arrived in 2003, Amylin was a small organization of a few hundred people. When she left in 2007, it was a force of more than 2,000.

Ginger impressed me on many levels. Her self-confidence was quite apparent as she spoke about her approach to leadership; like the others, she had a powerful inner compass guiding her. What struck me even more, however, was how self-reflective she was, able to question herself and own her vulnerability. This capacity reflected not uncertainty as many might imagine but an inner strength that allowed for honesty and truth. That strength supported her during a difficult time at a previous company when she felt forced to choose between her values and her job. In her words,

> *Thirteen years ago I was hired to run ACS, a medical device company owned by Eli Lilly, which also owned a huge conglomerate of companies. At the time, ACS was a cash flow generator for the device business, with potential for growth in a growing market and a long history of winning. Due to countless issues throughout Eli Lilly's network of properties, a mandate came down from corporate headquarters that there could be no raises in the next year. That, to me, was implausible. To grow a business, to attract innovative people, to reduce turnover, to fix problems, and to reignite growth in a profitable and high-tech business that helps people's lives, you can't freeze wages in Silicon Valley. And so I refused to comply and administered wage increases that next year. There was a moment when I thought I would lose my job over it, but it was the right thing to do and thankfully that didn't happen. Years later, I was reminded by someone of the huge impact it made on the people in the company because it was right for the business even though it didn't comply with the rules.*

The choice to stay true to one's values and beliefs is not something Ginger did as a calculated strategy. It was who she was, and this very fact is what stands her apart from so many others. How do I know this? Is there any research to substantiate this claim? Hardly. Yet look into your heart and ask yourself, What inspires you? If you can answer that question, then you will get a glimpse into the passion that drives such leaders as Ginger to take these kinds of risks. The only thing that continues to surprise me is how so few leaders are able to see this.

"Me, Too" Values

Throughout my career, I have often been asked to help companies get clear about their core values. Ever since the best-selling book *Corporate Cultures* came out in 1982 (written by my doctoral advisor, Terry Deal, and Allen Kennedy), companies have been espousing the importance of values—whether or not they actually practice them. I believe that well over half the companies in the United States have values statements, expressed in some form. You can see them nicely written and framed on walls, written on coffee mugs, and pasted on placards. I do not believe that there are this many companies whose behavior truly lines up with these values. Unfortunately, too many leaders see values as a means to an end, pieces to move on a profit-seeking chessboard. They treat values as objects to have as opposed to immovable ways of being. This causes a huge gap between what is said and what is done. Andrall Pearson, a former President of PepsiCo and Harvard Business School professor once said that the gap between espoused values and actually living them is "the largest single source of cynicism and skepticism in the workplace today." Is it any wonder that so many people continue to long for great leaders?

The leaders of the companies depicted in that book, however, along with others like them, don't treat values as objects to own and manipulate; they live them, and in so doing inspire powerful cultures to form naturally around them. Like Ginger Graham, the leaders I met seem to hold their values as more precious than gold. Their flame burns bright not so much for what they do but for how they carry themselves when the chips are down. And I suspect the same is true for most every remarkable leader throughout the world. All are willing to live their values under the greatest hardship. You can't buy such values because their source is internally generated, and they can't be "used" to achieve other aims, although organizations and leaders keep trying.

I am reminded of an extraordinary event that occurred almost 15 years ago that defined what I mean. On December 11, 1995, a fire burned most of Malden Mills to the ground, threatening to put its 3000 employees permanently out of work. While in the parking lot, bemoaning their seeming inevitable fate, a few of the employees heard the sole owner and CEO, Aaron Feuerstein, say, "this is not the end." Spending literally millions of his own hard earned money, Feuerstein kept all 3000 employees on the payroll with full benefits for 3 months until the Mill could get back on its feet. When asked why he made such an extraordinary choice, he said, "I have a responsibility to the worker, both blue-collar and white-collar...and I have an equal responsibility to the community. It would have been unconscionable to put 3000 people on the streets and deliver a deathblow to our surrounding cities. Maybe on paper our company is worth less to Wall Street, but I can tell you it's worth more." When asked about his motives, he said plainly and clearly, "The fundamental difference [between me and most other leaders] is that I consider our workers an asset, not an expense."[2]

The differentiator in this context for me is simple. Many leaders say those words but when push comes to shove, they don't mean them. Aaron Feuerstein did and his choice was not really a choice at all, it was an act that was a direct extension of who he was. The real test of a leader is not what he or she says, but what he or she does.

When ambition drives values, those values are empty because inauthentic leaders will toss them out the window as soon as they "get in the way." Many consultants share the blame as they smell the money in the "values and vision clarification" game.

> *Too many leaders see values as a
> means to an end, pieces to move on
> a profit-seeking chessboard.*

There are multiple, often unexamined, problems embedded in the way that consultants guide clients in the process of clarifying values. For example, many consultants and leaders don't understand that the process of generating core values is not a *creative* one but one of *discovery*. Creativity, at its root, is about creating something from nothing. Brainstorming, for example, doesn't belong in the search for powerful core values because it relies on imagination to envision something new. The values that result from such a process may feel exciting and filled with promise, but participants can't really own them for they come from outside of themselves—such values lack the tensile strength of a natural inner resolve. A true core-values process takes people into their deepest selves to discover the values that live within. As an example, one of the processes I use in my consulting work asks people to identify five important events in their life that helped shape who they are today. The particular events they choose is less important than the meaning they attach to those events, which reveals the values that are already inside them. In choosing a specific event, they show its deeper role in their personal value system.

Another part of the problem is that too many consultants and leaders see values clarification as a consensus process. Believing the well-worn maxim that the best way to create "buy-in" is through a participatory process that includes everyone usually delivers a watered-down version of what could have been. Such values start to look the same no matter the company because, in order to satisfy everyone, you end up settling for common denominators that feel like lofty abstractions. Early in my career I was one of those very same consultants, and as a result my work lacked the depth that my clients needed. I have since come to believe that great visions and values are specific to the needs of a particular organization and the aspirations of those who work there, and they won't emerge from a one-size-fits-all process.

Because of these reasons I don't usually recommend a consensus process for clarifying or discovering vision and values. Instead, I often focus on the leaders of the future, not because of what they will get from the organization but for what they want to put into it. In other words, to clarify the company's values, I want to work with those people who are mission-driven and not just there to collect a paycheck. These are the ones who will drive the organization toward greatness.

And so the equation is really quite simple: If the search for a new vision and values that match is an objective that really matters, then take the time to find that inner compass. And if a company isn't willing to do that, then that objective never meant much in the first place. The values that emerge from a shortchanged process inevitably won't endure, and the people in the company will have another reason to lose faith in their leadership. No wonder the processes that so many companies go through generate so much cynicism.

For me these were hard-won lessons, and now when I work with leaders and companies who are committed to finding their inner compass, we take the time. We may head to the mountains or some isolated place far removed from the trappings of corporate life. There we explore not competitive landscapes or scenario-building balance sheets but the passions they have and the core of their values that ring so true that they want to shout them from the mountaintops. For in discovering this inner fire, one finally arrives at the center of their being. They find, in the words of Archimedes, "a place to stand." And equally important—they are willing to stand alone, as the American poet Javan suggests in *Maybe I Will Never Be*:

> *I'm not very good*
> *At this Game called Life*
> *For I've not learned to see children crying*
> *Without feeling pain*
> *For I've not learned to watch animals destroyed*
> *Without wondering why*

For I've not yet met a king or a celebrity
That I would bow down to
Or a man so insignificant
That I would use for a stepping stone
For I have not learned to be a "yes man"
To narrow-minded bosses
Who quote rules without reason
And I've not learned to manipulate
The feelings of others
To be used for my own advantages
Then cast aside as I see fit

No, I'm not very good
At this Game called Life
And if everything goes well
Maybe I never will be

When working with leaders around their core values, I will inevitably hear someone put down the process or the values discovered as being nothing more than motherhood and apple pie. And, ironically, that is what they are—grounded and enduring. All fundamental values run deep into the earth while reaching for the heavens. They are, indeed, as plain and natural as motherhood and apple pie, and there are dozens that apply. The key is discovering which values are true for you and/or your organization, and these can be quite specific. For one company, a caring ethic might be crucial to who they are. For another, it might be aggressive risk-taking. Whichever ones are appropriate, owning them provides clarity and focus. The leaders of great companies never scoff at their values or question their importance. To them, living their values is absolutely natural.

In a world where the bottom line is usually the measure of success, there are many who downplay the importance of values. After all, they might argue, we have a responsibility to our shareholders, and certain "values" can get in the way. These people tend to fall into two groups. The first includes those who are not in contact with their own core values, for if they had a powerful inner compass, they would recognize the significance of living with such integrity. The second group is populated by the cynics who have seen such claims to values violated by those they trusted. They feel lied to, cheated, and betrayed. I often sense, though, that underneath the cynic's mask is a deeper desire to live in integrity and for others to do the same. If we strip away that mask, we might find a tender, wounded person inside who desperately seeks a life of meaning.

There is an Italian saying that speaks directly to the heart of the issue: *Tra il dire e il fare, ce in mezzo il mare*, which means, "There is an ocean between saying and doing." And in many organizations, this is the unfortunate truth. I think back to something Ginger Graham said to me: "What is integrity? In the end, it's just a set of behaviors. You can say you're honest and reliable, but if you never come through then how can I believe you? The hardest test of all is just doing what you say you'll do and holding yourself to the same standard that you hold other people to." Such is the nature of the golden flame. It burns bright not by mouthing intentions but by bridging the ocean between the saying and the doing.

Moments of Truth

Years ago, Jan Carlzon, then the admired leader of Scandinavian Airlines, wrote a simple but profound book on leadership called *Moments of Truth*.[3] In it he described life in an organization as an endless series of difficult choices. At each point you are faced with a moment of truth. Which road do you take? Organizations and people that are truly inspired keep choosing to honor their values moment by moment, a recurrent theme among the leaders I interviewed. And while there may be sacrifices in making such decisions, much more is ultimately gained, including the building of one's inner strength and of relationships based on trust. In the words of Chris Chavez,

> *I've come to the conclusion that there are a lot of smart people in the world, but when it comes to showing your true colors, it takes courage to do the right thing. Even when it hurts, if you can do what is right, knowing that*

you will pay a price, to me that is the ultimate in moral courage, and the ultimate in leadership.

Pat Tillman, a star football player for the Arizona Cardinals who threw fame and fortune away to support the U.S. mission in Iraq, comes to mind. He died for a cause that mattered to him more than the sport he loved. So did Abraham Lincoln and Mahatma Gandhi, who lost their lives in a fight for freedom, for a cause greater than themselves. Those who have made the biggest difference in the world had values that couldn't be shaken. For without being grounded in oneself and one's stance in the world, you are vulnerable to the choices of others, which can lead to victimhood or a retreat into cynicism and mistrust. And when this happens, your chance to have meaningful impact will be lost.

A good friend of mine, Scotty, was the CEO of a startup business with a partner who had invented a product for the sporting goods industry. While the product was truly revolutionary, Scotty had enormous difficulty with his partner, who was mercurial and capricious. Too often, it seemed to Scotty, the inventor behaved toward potential customers and suppliers in ways that were slippery and dishonest. Nevertheless, he put two years of full-time sweat equity into the company, trying to grow the business and getting it to the point where it was poised for breakthrough success. Along the way, he also worked hard to help the inventor change his patterns of behavior. As a result of his efforts and some modest investment capital, he earned a majority ownership in the firm with the rest going to his partner.

Unfortunately, as much as Scotty tried to develop a reasonably healthy relationship with this partner, he had made little headway. Finally, he decided that the best thing to do, for himself, for his partner, and for the business, was to leave the company despite his concern that, if he left, the company would fail and he would have nothing for his invested time and money. In an extraordinary act of generosity, he decided to give all of his stock in the company to his partner as a Christmas gift. This enabled his now former partner to find another partner with executive experience who could lead the company toward fulfilling its potential. Scotty was barely eking out a living at the time and may have left over a million dollars on the table as a result of this extraordinary decision, if and when the company gets bought out. But to him the reasoning was simple (though not easy). Faced with either going for the money or living a life consistent with his values, he chose his values.

I'm working with a company that is in the middle of transforming itself. In this process the leadership has set forth a powerful and compelling vision, including a set of values to guide the company and the efforts of the people in it. Like any such process there is evidence of movement forward, and there are also people unwilling to embrace the change. In this particular case, one of those in resistance is a top leader whose behavior, most everyone agrees, isn't consistent with the values. Nevertheless, the head of the company is reluctant to fire this person. This has led some to question the leader's willingness to act on his own values.

The company's employees, knowing all this, are starting to feel stuck. They are blaming the leader and the one in resistance, losing confidence that the vision has any meaning, and concluding that the new values are empty. I counseled the employees that, regardless of the CEO's motives, they should consider their own stance in the matter. What are *your* values? What is *your* purpose? What does *your* compass say? If you don't have an internal map to guide you, you end up feeling powerless to do anything other than to complain that others aren't behaving the way you want them to. A far more self-empowering stance is to get clear about who you are and what you stand for, and then make your choices. And if your internal compass calls for you to confront the situation, do so. If your internal compass calls for you to have compassion and to seek further understanding, that too would be appropriate, as long as the decision comes from your core of who you are.

Great leadership, then, is largely about choices. Do I live my life consistent with my purpose and values or do I let lesser needs and ambitions drive me? Put differently, the choice is between what Carl

> *Great leadership is largely about choices. Do I live my life consistent with my purposes and values?*

Jung referred to as the higher Self or larger self—which he signified by capitalizing the word *Self,* and the smaller *self,* which is often referred to as one's ego. Do I do that which serves the greater good or do I serve only myself?

Moments of truth are not just for leaders holding important positions of power. Anyone can demonstrate acts of great leadership in any given moment by making tough choices and living their values. I recently attended a meeting of the top 35 leaders of a large and growing multinational corporation. At one point a group of leaders in one division were discussing their concerns about another division and its performance. Rather than voice those concerns directly, though, they kept dancing around the issue, saying things like, "We could use more focus" or "You folks are great, it's just that we need a little more." Cheryl, the head of the division being discussed, kept asking questions to try to clarify their feedback, but the responses remained vague, as if no one wanted to upset her or any of the others in the room. Cheryl knew what they were trying to say, but felt frustrated that they wouldn't just come out and say it. Finally she said, "You guys keep beating around the bush. I think you're trying to say that we don't have a strong work ethic and it troubles you." She paused to gauge their reaction. A few said "Yes" and others nodded their heads. Cheryl didn't hesitate. She looked each one in the eye and responded with conviction, "Well, I think you are absolutely right!" Then they all nodded yes and began talking about the impact on them. Cheryl's actions turned the meeting around.

In taking this stand, Cheryl did two things. She challenged the group by saying, "Let's be direct and honest here. Nothing less will be okay with me." And she also demonstrated that when feedback is given, it needs to be taken in. When those two conditions are met, words meet action and issues can start moving toward resolution.

Later in the meeting, Cheryl pointed out that she believed that this leadership group too often skirted important issues. "From here on forward," she challenged them, "let's not walk past a problem." The phrase implied that when a value such as work ethic is violated, the issue needs to be addressed immediately. This dictum has since become a mantra for the company's leaders. Now they are committed to facing and discussing difficult issues, and in so doing, both the company and the people who work there are finding it easier to keep walking the talk.

The phrase itself makes a difference, but what made it penetrate the meeting was the behavior of the person who voiced it. Cheryl showed leadership qualities that day by stepping up and meeting a challenge with courage and integrity. What makes this even more noteworthy is that, among those attending, Cheryl was a junior executive. She could have just allowed the others to drive the meeting and kept quiet. But she didn't. She was willing to speak her truth no matter the consequences, and as a result everyone benefited.

There can be much at stake in such moments of truth. One of the remarkable leaders I met had dreamed for most of his adult life of becoming the CEO of a large company. For ten years he assiduously worked his way up the corporate ladder of a major corporation until he was eventually offered the position of president. However, upon learning that the existing CEO had planned to deploy a number of unethical strategies and tactics in the coming months, this leader turned down the offer and left the company. Not only was it the job of a lifetime, almost inevitably leading him to the CEO position he had wanted, he walked away from more than $10 million. Instead he became the CEO of a much smaller company, which eventually became an industry leader while winning numerous awards. In looking back, he says he has never regretted his decision. Honoring his integrity was a far more important source of wealth.

Many of the leaders I met on my journey chose integrity over some lesser value despite the likely loss of money or status or security. In so doing, they gained enormous satisfaction in knowing that their actions ended up having a positive impact in the world. Their flame turned golden by virtue of those choices, and with each new impeccable choice, that flame burned ever brighter.

Integrity and Courage

On the surface it may appear that great leadership requires great courage, and to some extent that may be true. But I believe that most of the leaders I met would not describe themselves as courageous. They would probably refer to someone who had died in battle as being truly courageous. For them, making difficult decisions when faced with moments of truth isn't courage but doing the only thing they know how to do—following their internal guidance system and living by their own code. In meeting these remarkable leaders, I have come to believe that acting with integrity is not a choice for them, as it seems for so many others. They don't use values as if they are objects to own and ration out; they *are* their values. When someone embodies their values in this way, the decisions they make don't represent courage; they reflect basic acts of integrity that come from being integrated within oneself.

One of the reasons why we are so consistently disappointed with our elected officials is that while they talk about service to "God and country," their ambition for the position often reflects a desire to serve their ego—the little self. And much of the time, the most ambitious go the farthest. They will do what it takes—whatever the system demands—to get elected, even if that means to lie and cheat.

This, of course, isn't true of all elected officials. Harry S. Truman was arguably the last honest American President. He was admired by many not just for his deft and courageous leadership but also because he was trusted. He never really sought the presidency. He assumed the position after only a few months as vice president when Franklin Roosevelt died. And prior to the election that followed, he resisted the call to run. He didn't like being President and his wife never felt comfortable in the White House. But his sense of duty to the needs of the country outweighed his personal preference, and he won by a modest margin. Because he knew he wouldn't run again, his tenure was marked by courageous decision-making and an uncompromising dedication to forthrightness. In other words, he led from his purpose all the way, and in so doing distinguished himself as one of the finest leaders of the 20th century. It will be interesting to watch how the new U.S. President, Barack Obama, who campaigned on a platform of integrity and consistency, delivers on his promises when facing the many difficult decisions that await him.

One Leader's Process of Becoming a Leader of Integrity

I began working with Arnold a couple of years ago. He is a young, talented leader of a rapidly growing company who nevertheless felt that something wasn't right. He called me and asked for some guidance.

In exploring the issue with him, I began to see a man who was very courageous, having started his company from scratch and bootstrapping it into a $50 million business, and yet was still unwilling to fully embrace who he was and what he believed in. He had a set of values that he deeply held, but he also knew that he was compromising those values in the service of continued growth, afraid to put his company at risk.

We spent a day in the mountains to see if we could find what resonated in his heart and to gain clarity about what he needed to do. We explored the important choices he had made throughout his life that shaped who he was today. We also went through a number of reflective processes designed to reveal the deepest levels of what he stood for.

In a series of subsequent meetings, we explored the many moments when he faced a choice between what he knew to be his values and what he thought was prudent for the company. Often Arnold chose to act with integrity but like us all, he sometimes chose to violate his core principles. For each situation, we explored the outcome both for him personally and for his business. He began to see that he wasn't leading with the courage and conviction he knew was there, and that the price he was paying for those compromised moments was too great. Finally, he made a bold choice.

Arnold took his executive team offsite to consider the next steps for the company. He admitted his mistakes, but he also put a stake in the ground—his days of compromising were over. If this meant that people would leave the company or that he would have to let someone go, so be it. What happened was magical: Each member of the team admitted to his or her own transgressions and vowed to join him, and ever since, the company has continued on a path of success. From a business standpoint, nothing had changed; the basic operations remained the same. From a longer-term perspective, however, everything changed, because the company and this leader, coming together in a spirit of teamwork and honesty, tapped their potential for being a leader in their industry. Perhaps not surprisingly, this didn't really matter to Arnold. Sure, he was proud that the company was successfully moving forward, but more importantly, he was now living his life in a way that he could feel good about.

The role of values and choice cannot be overemphasized in shaping a life that has integrity at the core. An old legend has it that, as a young man, William Penn (the future first Governor of Pennsylvania) was exploring the possibility of adopting the Quaker religion.[4] For years he had worn a sword, as was the custom of his time. In once using it to save his life, he justified his behavior by quoting Christ, who had said, "He that hath no sword, let him sell his garment and buy one." Yet in considering the Quaker religion as a path for his increasingly peaceful ways, he became troubled by this custom; the Quakers were devoutly committed to inner peace and love. Young William was concerned that if he continued to wear the sword, he would stand out among them. He sought the counsel of George Fox, a devout Quaker. "What should I do?" young William asked George. Fox's answer likely surprised him: "I advise thee to wear [your sword] as long as thou canst." It clearly states one of the principle tenets of Quakerism—to honor one's own inner guidance system rather than following existing strictures or the opinions of others.

A short time later they met again. In noticing that William had no sword, George asked, "William, where is thy sword?" "Oh!" replied William, "I took thy advice, and wore it as long as I could." Which wasn't very long, as the tension between his inner counsel and his actions became unbearable. Such is the path of self-awareness and choice for all great leaders. They choose not because they are told to but only after listening to the wisdom within.

While the choice to act with integrity appears courageous to many, to the remarkable leader it is not. It is simply an act born from a desire to be congruent with what is felt from the core. The stronger the values that are anchored to that core, the stronger the tension when they aren't being met. That tension is relieved when making new choices which honor those values. This is integrity, and it leads to a feeling of deep alignment. From the story of William Penn and others, one can see the simple progression from desire to right action:

| Deep Values out of alignment | Unbearable Tension | New Choices | Deep Values in alignment |

Figure 5-1: The Path to Alignment

Achieving one's own unique leadership potential, then, requires acting on values that come to light through inner awareness. Too often we live in a state of numbness, unaware of our own internal tensions. Oblivious to these deeper currents, we justify our choices, act out of integrity, and wonder why we feel so little satisfaction.

Aligning one's values and actions isn't easy, for values often compete with one other. For example, I have long lived under the illusion that I am committed to contributing toward a sustainable planet. I speak publicly about my care, and I take some actions that align with it, such as recycling and energy conservation. At the same time, my lifestyle has been typical of those who believe in the American dream of acquisition and achievement. I've worked hard to get to where I am, I (we) say, and I deserve what that brings me. Witness the number of politicians who, in response to suggestions to protect our environment, assert, "We cannot do that. It will threaten our standard of living!" And yet we rarely question the underlying assumptions embedded in this belief. Up until recently, we've been unwilling to examine how the modern lifestyle, claimed by millions, is contributing to the crippling of the planet. Our (my) values of consumption, convenience, and abundance are thus in direct conflict with the value of sustainability.

For me this is a dawning realization, and in response, rather than go numb or deny the conflict, I have chosen to feel the tension and it's becoming unbearable. As it does so, however, I notice that I'm making some radical choices to reduce my impact and live a life in accordance with planetary sustainability. Sure, this requires some sacrifices, but in making these choices I am starting to experience a deeper level of integration and integrity. This is not so much about honesty as it is about wholeness— bringing all of our actions and ourselves into alignment with our core values. And this sense of alignment naturally results in caring about something beyond oneself. It is to this subject of care—not just of individuals, but also of humanity as a whole—that we now turn.

KEY POINTS IN CHAPTER 5

- The best leaders are anchored in their values. It is from this that they earn the trust of others.

- When it comes to values, you can't pick and choose your spots.

- You cannot copy another's values and expect to become a great leader.

- You cannot create values; you must discover them.

- Every moment is a moment of truth.

CHAPTER 6

✧

CARING AS A PASSION

*I don't know what your destiny will be, but
one thing I do know: The only ones among
you who will be really happy are those who
have sought and found how to serve.*
—Albert Schweitzer

Sometimes the most everyday, seemingly routine exchanges can inspire far beyond their apparent significance. Recently I came into contact with a van driver, and what followed, although quite ordinary in one sense, was particularly poignant. For whatever reason, on that day, at that moment in time, my heart was open to receiving what this person had to offer, something simple and altogether beautiful.

Paul Crug works for Park & Fly, Inc., a large company that owns and operates parking lots near airports and transports passengers to and from the lot and the airport. On this particular day, Paul picked me up in the Park & Fly van. He greeted me with a smile and a friendly "welcome" as he lifted my suitcase into the van. He did the same with each of the other passengers, in a way that wasn't perfunctory but heartfelt, his warmth palpable. As he took us from the airport to the lot, he drove past someone waiting for another transport service to arrive and pick him up. Paul immediately slowed down and, his eyes peering back at us in the rearview mirror, announced, "Poor guy, he's been there for a while. I know this may slow you all down a bit, but do you mind if I pick him up?" No one spoke against it, distracted by their thoughts or tired from their travels, and he did so, getting out of his driver's seat to help the person up the steps. As we drove off, Paul stated in a cheerful voice, "Hey, I know you're all tired. We'll be there in eight minutes." A bit later, gesturing out the window, he let us know, "There's a Citgo gas station right around the corner. If you need gas, they will give you what you need." And so it went for that short trip to the lot—one helpful bit of information after another.

Appreciating his deep desire to be of service, I wondered about the effect he was having on the other passengers. As I looked around the van, it appeared that they were simply ignoring him, but Paul didn't seem to mind. His friendliness not only seemed genuine, it was not dependent on constant acknowledgment from others. When we arrived at the lot, he dropped everyone off and carried their bags to their cars, offering a smile and a sincere "Thank you."

I was the last person off and was moved to tell him how much I appreciated his attitude. He smiled, grateful for the acknowledgment. I asked him if he is like this all the time, and he replied in a matter-of-fact manner, "Well, I guess I am. I just like people. I always have."

Paul Crug was truly an inspiration that day. He was alive with feeling and maintained a constant spirit of service to others. His deep caring showed up not as a concept but as something tangible. He touched my heart, and as I drove home, I wondered about the degree to which *I* care like that. I remembered moments of my life when I clearly didn't. For example, when I've forgotten the names of people I've met, I send a message that "I don't care enough about you to remember your name." Similarly, when people have come to my home, I've often neglected to be a good host, expecting them to take care of themselves. I may let people know, "mi casa es su casa," which seems gracious enough, but rarely have I gone the extra distance. I know in my heart that I care, but as I live my daily life, moving from task to task and idea to idea, I become disconnected from this feeling. My ambitions can get in the way. I forget what Paul Crug seemed to know instinctively: Deep caring is fundamental to life. It's the simple connections with others that matter, reminding us that we are not alone.

Many of the leaders I've met in my journey do *not* forget. Caring is in the foreground of their lives, not something incidental that they occasionally remind themselves to do. Their loving attention shows up in ways both obvious and subtle. For example, I was deeply moved the moment I met Scott Johnson, the leader of a nonprofit organization called The Myelin Repair Foundation, dedicated to changing the landscape of research and treatment of multiple sclerosis. Scott has been afflicted with the condition for over 30 years.

Years ago Scott made his living as a business consultant while keeping up with the research on MS. After awhile he concluded that few medical researchers understood the condition from a holistic perspective. Each had his or her own theory or perspective, and tended to analyze the condition by breaking it down into tiny parts. Scott realized that MS is a knotty medical problem and much more systemic in nature. Breaking the problem into parts and working on each one separately, as is customary in the medical field, didn't make sense to him. Instead, he intuitively believed the problem should be approached through collaboration among many researchers in hopes that their shared effort might reveal unique perspectives and solutions. Hence, the Myelin Repair Foundation was born. Scott's intention goes well beyond MS, though. Ultimately, he intends to revolutionize the way all major medical conditions do research.

I arrived at Scott's modest office in Saratoga, CA. Upon seeing me enter, he immediately got out of his chair, hobbled across the room, greeted me with a warm smile, and asked if he could get me anything. "A soft drink or some water, perhaps?" I asked for some water, assuming he would ask his assistant to get it. He did not. He slowly walked to another room to get me what I'd asked for. His graciousness was more than memorable; it showed genuine care.

With few exceptions, each of the leaders I met showed this level of care. It was always about people, but not always in the same way. For some, it came in the form of tender love. Jerry Jampolsky expressed this trait beautifully when he said, "If I could name the primary quality of a good leader, it would be holding everyone's heart gently." In others, the care showed up in the form of believing in people and creating conditions where they could live up to their potential. And sometimes such caring shows up on a larger canvas, for example, as a concern for the well-being of humankind, expressed in the many ways that leaders contribute to others in need. Scott Johnson's vision for accelerating the search for effective treatments of MS comes immediately to mind.

> *With few exceptions, each of the leaders I met showed this level of care.*

Most importantly, the effort must be authentic regardless of the persons or causes the care is aimed toward. Too often I hear leaders invite others to participate in making a decision so that they will "feel" included. The best leaders don't want to create just a feeling, though. They want to create something that is *real* and for their employees to feel that realness. Chris Chavez of Advanced Neuromodulation Systems described it well when he said that his greatest desire is to leave behind a powerful legacy in which people are uplifted by his work. With regard to authentic leadership, he said

> *The people in the organization you lead can read your mind. They can read your heart. You may fool them for a little bit, but you can never fool them forever. So ultimately I think leaders have to care. They have to care about the people they lead. They have to care about the customers that they're trying to serve. They have to be visibly sincere. They have to walk the talk.*

Never Walk Past Anyone

One of the leaders I met on my journey, Atef Mankarios, told me a story that spoke volumes about who he is and what he cares about. Atef runs a consulting firm called Mankarios Partners. Before starting his company, he was twice the leader of a chain of five-star hotels. He and his partners now help others build, staff, and run such hotels throughout the world. Atef sees his staff not as employees but as partners, and as you would with any "partner," you treat them with dignity and respect. He feels strongly that to be an aloof leader is to be no leader at all. He figures that if you are an employee of his hotel or his company, you are a partner and part of the team, and deserving of the utmost respect. That is his signature impact as a leader, and it rang loud and clear throughout our meeting. And from the story he told me, it was easy to see that this spirit of caring had deep roots.

In his early years in the hotel industry, Atef promised himself that if he ever became a manager, he would always remember his roots in the entry-level ranks of the profession. And so when he finally achieved his goal, Atef would greet his employees by making meaningful eye contact with each one. Among those he saw regularly was a gentleman from Ethiopia whose sole responsibility was to make the lobby shine. For well over two decades, this man dusted and polished every pillar and post, doorknob and desk lamp, with deep care and enormous pride, knowing that when the interior lobby shines, it creates an inviting luminosity for its guests.

Some days Atef would see the man sitting alone in a seat in the cafeteria, and he would walk up to sit and chat, perhaps over a cup of coffee, always thanking him for his good work. Each time after greeting him, Atef noticed that the man was sitting more upright or standing a bit taller, appreciating the kind words and energy that these greetings and conversations provided.

One day Atef sat a bit longer with the man, and was moved to ask about his life. Where had he come from, and how had he gotten to America? Cautiously at first, the man began to tell his story. It turned out that he was a professor of chemistry with a PhD at the top university in his country. He had come to America over 20 years ago as a refugee seeking a job teaching chemistry and chasing the mythical American Dream. Although blessed with intelligence and great resolve, he struggled to find work. For reasons that he could not fathom, opportunities in this "land of opportunity" were scarce. He often thought that the color of his skin or the fact that he was from another country was an impediment. As his limited funds began to run out, he started looking for any job he could get. He applied for positions as a waiter, a security guard, and for numerous other semiskilled positions. He was repeatedly turned down, usually because he was viewed as "overqualified." Just as his finances reached rock bottom, he secured the job that he now still held, some 20 years later. He was grateful to the hotel that hired him, fearing that he could do no better. So he stayed, carefully polishing, dusting, and sweeping, year after year, treating this job as if it were the only one he would ever have.

Atef was deeply moved by this man's story and vowed never to walk past anyone as so many had done with this fellow, observed by many yet known to few. Each person, no matter who they are, has a story to tell, and each employee has a special place in the great effort that was Atef's hotel. Now, despite all of his successes and ambitions, Atef believes that his primary contribution to the world has been to uphold the vow he made after hearing that story—to honor and respect everyone. This practice is Atef's sacred gift, and it defines him to this day.

Anchored in Deep Care

In addition to a core set of values that act as one's guide, having an inner anchor has to do with knowing what one cares about in the world and being true to that caring. I am reminded of the movie *City Slickers*, where Billy Crystal's character, Mitch, is alone with Curly, the gruff cowboy played by Jack Palance. Curly asks Mitch, "Do you know what the secret of life is?" Curly holds up one finger and says, "One thing. Just one thing. You stick to that and the rest don't mean s***." Mitch asks, "But what is the one thing?" Curly's reply is prophetic: "That's what you have to find out."

Kartar Singh Kalsa, the CEO of Golden Temple, a company that provides products in the health food industry, was clear about his one thing:

> *The mission of our company is to develop products [that] bring some enhancement to life, some enrichment, some positive quality. The business is oriented around that.*

Working with us is always something that our employees enjoy. They don't necessarily think about it all the time, but we get feedback that tells me it is true...Our business is great because of the connection and relationships we have with other people...The ultimate is when you can serve something bigger than yourself and feel joy in your life.

To a person, the remarkable leaders I met were unabashedly clear about what was most important to them. The phrasing and meaning were different in each case, but the conviction was always the same. One leader would say something like, "I am all about people." Another might say that, "we are here to redefine the industry or concept or profession." A third might say that, "in the end, it's all about love." Their goals were diverse, but there was no mistaking the fact that each one *knew* what they considered most important, and in this knowing they could rest comfortably with their choices.

> *The remarkable leaders I met were unabashedly clear about what was most important to them.*

That each of the leaders I met cared so deeply and was so relentless in his or her cause showed me the power and promise of living a soulful life. It wasn't just a matter of living in integrity, although that was a part of it. They cared for something that had meaning beyond themselves as individuals. And they placed that which they cared about before anything or anyone else. Chris Chavez said it well when he stated,

I've always thought about who I am as a leader. I think leadership is a privilege, an honor. It's not something you should aspire to for your own end. With leadership comes the awesome responsibility to do the right thing. There is

a difference between people who lead with purpose and a cause in mind and those who lead with a self-serving agenda. Our mission as a company is to help the millions of people who are suffering from chronic pain by making our products smarter, faster, smaller, more affordable, more functional, and more available.

"[Fill in the blank] matters to me," they each said, in different words. "No kidding, this really matters, so much so that I will throw everything else away if I have to. This is my soul's desire. And I will persist, no matter what." Mary Taverna, president of Hospice of Marin in California, powerfully expressed such a commitment when she described to me what it took to get the U.S. healthcare system to recognize the value of hospice care.

Over the months we became very involved with the direct care of the patients, in perfecting pain and symptom management, learning as much as we could about what people really needed at the end of life, understanding and appreciating the value of the family system, caring not just for one person but for whole families. There are social issues, spiritual issues, practical issues, and physical issues—there are all kinds of things going on at this time because everybody who cares about the person who's ill is affected. There was a big learning curve just figuring out how to do the work, not to mention overcoming the resistance that existed within the healthcare delivery system. As you go through this world and know something is truly right, the more resistance there seems to be. Knowing we were doing something right and caring so deeply about our cause, we were compelled to break that resistance down, particularly on the part of physicians. And slowly, one by one, they began to see the value of this type of care.

Seeing with More than Eyes

One of the most inspiring meetings I had on my journey was with Gordon Gund, an accomplished leader and business owner. Gordon is an entrepreneur who has started and owned multiple businesses, some of which failed, many of which succeeded. He was the former owner of several professional sports teams and a classified ad company (Nationwide Advertising) with offices throughout the country. He has been chairman of the board of the National Basketball Association, the builder of the Gund Arena (now the Quicken Loans Arena) that houses the Cleveland Cavaliers, the co-founder of The Foundation Fighting Blindness, co-founder and partner with his lifelong friend Hugh Scott of Gus Enterprises, a successful real estate development and management company headquartered in San Francisco, and the founder-leader of a venture capital firm that has spawned many promising companies.

But though he has started and led many successful businesses, making him worthy of respect, this is not what makes him a great leader. There are two things about Gordon that cause him to stand head and shoulders above the competition. First, his sense of integrity and commitment to others is beyond reproach. And second (though he may disagree with this one), he has been completely blind since the age of 31.

His blindness was caused by an unusual affliction called retinitis pigmentosa, which took his eyesight in the late 1960s. It began when he started having trouble seeing at night. At the time an ophthalmologist dismissed his concerns, telling him that people with his condition usually maintain their sight well into their sixties. But fate took a severe turn shortly thereafter, and in a span of six months, Gordon lost all his sight except for a central tube of vision, like looking through a straw.

Exhausting all treatment avenues in the United States, Gordon heard about an experimental form of therapy being tried in Russia. Although the Cold War was then at its height, he was determined to gain back his vision in any way he could, so he departed for Russia with his brother. What was expected to be a stay of just a few days, however, turned out to be a fateful six weeks. In addition to the bureaucratic challenges of travel during that time, his brother had to return to the States sooner than he expected.

Gordon remained at the treatment facility where no one spoke English and communication became very difficult. As he describes below, it was in a state of futility, exasperation, and hopelessness—with a keen awareness that his eyesight might never return—that he came to discover the true meaning of his life:

> *While in Russia, I didn't have people I could complain to or lean on to help me avoid facing the fact of what I was dealing with and what it would mean to my life. So I had to look inside myself and think about what really mattered. And I hit rock bottom, no question about it. But I did find bedrock in my love for my family and friends, and in my desire to take what I had left in terms of capabilities and maximize those in my roles as a husband and a father, as a friend, and as an entrepreneur so that I could build on the things I had rather than thinking about what I'd lost.*
>
> *To do this I was going to have to learn to depend on people, to ask them for help, and at the same time— because it's very important to me—to be able to help them.*
>
> *The basic premise of my life is that I want to enjoy what I'm doing and I want the people around me to enjoy doing it with me. And I want them to grow and to feel they are empowered and that they are important to our common mission or strategic goal.*

In a situation when many people might focus solely on their predicament and become a passive and helpless victim of their circumstance, Gordon got in touch with his core values and intensified and clarified his commitments—and this has defined his life ever since. He decided to not make his affliction a barrier and instead dedicated his life to making a difference. His experience reminded me of the Greek sea god

Proteus, who was capable of changing shape in response to a crisis. How often have the qualities of resilience, adaptability, and creativity played a pivotal role in our lives?

As our conversation continued, Gordon repeatedly emphasized the central questions that have come to define his commitment and leadership: What difference am I making? Am I being true to my values of honesty and forthrightness? Am I contributing to the learning and well-being of others? These questions shape and define both his professional and personal life, so that there is no distinction between them.

As a blind man, Gordon has no choice but to depend on and trust others for help in a wide range of areas that most of us take for granted. He has come to realize that to trust others fully, he also needs to act in a trustworthy manner. And so for Gordon, it all comes down to integrity—to act with the utmost integrity in all of his dealings, and to expect others to do the same.

Toward the end of our meeting together, Gordon said something to me that revealed the depth of who he is. "You know, Keith," he said, "because I'm blind, I can't see what people look like when I meet them. Their size, shape, weight, and the color of their skin—all are completely unknown to me. As a result I have no way of prejudging them. I make decisions about people based on my experience of them in the moment. I can tell whether they act in a trustworthy manner by their behavior and the tone of their voice. Appearances don't matter to me, so I can cut through a lot of the inner noise [their conscious or unconscious prejudices] that others unconsciously deal with."

Follow Your Desire

Of all the things that each of these leaders cared about, the one that stood out the most for me (perhaps because I wanted to see it or because it seems so rare) was their passionate desire for others to follow *their* own inner compass. Almost without exception, they felt they were following their own compass and now their attention was on helping others to do the same. I believe that each and every living thing is imbued with an essential and unique nature—an expression of our soul. Addressing the issue of trying to live by others' rules or by a light that isn't your own, Joseph Campbell, the great Jungian interpreter of the world's myths, said, "Whenever a knight of the Grail tried to follow a path made by someone else, he went altogether astray. Where there is a way or path, it is someone else's footsteps. Each of us has to find our own way."[1] When we are following our deepest desire, we are lit up with life. We then embody the golden flame. (We will explore this notion in more detail in Chapter 9.)

> *"Living one's soul" means living life consistent with one's deepest desires.*

Go All The Way

When Paul Centenari and his brother bought the Atlas Container Corporation in 1988, it was a fading company that seemed to be going nowhere. Based on its condition, you would not call this a turnaround effort. Instead, it appeared more like an effort to give life support to a slowly dying patient. For most of his life, Paul dreamed of running a company. He never imagined it would be one like this, but in his dreams it included one simple notion—that people ought to have a say in the conditions and decisions that affect them directly. Motivated by this vision, he saw a potential in Atlas Container that sparked him to buy the company.

What Atlas Container does isn't rocket science. They make boxes and other containers for shipping purposes. It's a low-margin, blue-collar kind of business that is very difficult to make solvent and even more difficult to make prosperous. But prosperous it has become. When Paul bought the company, its revenues were $5.5 million. In 2008, it was $65 million. Paul would tell you that the key to the improvement was the implementation of a governing and decision-making process that could best be described as extreme organizational democracy.

Paul believes in the wisdom and power of a group to make intelligent decisions. "Often," he said, "I have the belief that my decision or judgment is best, either because I have thought it through more than others, or because I have more information or knowledge. But that is an illusion. Who am I to judge what is best for others? So we vote on things, and we abide by the vote. Even if I disagree with it or it's not the best decision on paper, I've got to go along because the fact that the group decided to do it generates a far stronger commitment than if I had made the decision alone. I'm willing to risk making poor decisions as a group from time to time in return for powerful commitment."

It is Paul's trust in the people of the organization, and the trust they return, that yield such extraordinary results. His leadership is defined by deep caring—about people, about ideas, and about the power of people to turn ideas into reality.

The lesson I take away from all of this is that, ultimately, whether you or I become a remarkable leader defined by deep caring has everything to do with the choices we make in each moment of our lives. All people, whether they are in positions of power or not, are faced with a choice. We influence all the time, and people in positions of power, in particular, influence in significant ways. What we choose reflects our ideals and the promises we make to ourselves for how we will live our life. We can choose to live from a fear of scarcity or from a commitment to abundance for all.

> *...whether you or I become a remarkable leader defined by deep caring has everything to do with the choices we make in each moment of our lives.*

I am reminded of the story of King Minos and the Bull. In the story, King Minos begins as a decent man who does not seize the recently vacated throne of Crete through force, trickery or deceit, as do so many rulers in Greek mythology, but by turning to Poseidon, the sea-God, for guidance. As a result, Poseidon honors Minos' humility by bestowing upon him the throne. This gift from the gods reminds us of...

> ...the ancient symbolism of kingship, which has always portrayed the king as a vessel for deity, a kind of 'good shepherd' who rules his people through the grace of God and renews his power through the renewal of his vow to serve.[2]

Unfortunately, the story of King Minos ends with him betraying the trust of Poseidon. In addition to the gift of power, Poseidon gave Minos a bull from the sea as a sign that Minos' claim to the throne was favored by divine powers. In return, Poseidon had Minos agree that he would affirm his loyalty to Poseidon by later sacrificing this bull back to Poseidon.

Minos, however, allowed his greed and vanity to take over and kept the extraordinary bull for breeding. He sent his second-best bull to Poseidon instead. Of course, the god was angry and punished Minos by causing his wife to fall in love with the bull from the sea. From their union, the Minotaur was born, a half human, half bull beast that for years dined on the flesh of children. Eventually, the Athenian hero Theseus kills the Minotaur and became the ruler of Athens and Crete. Minos died of sorrow and guilt—his betrayal of Poseidon corrupted his kingship at the very core.

Referring to the story of King Minos, the words of Liz Greene and Juliet Sharman-Burke echo strongly in my heart. In their book, *The Mythic Journey*, they explain that the story of King Minos...

> ... teaches us that handling power with integrity is not simply something we do publicly to impress others. It is an inner commitment to whatever we choose to call God, whether we use religious terminology or the more objective language of humanitarian concerns. If the commitment is sincere, and we keep loyal to the dictates of our hearts, then we renew our inner power and authenticity. If we are hypocrites, we may fool some, but we

cannot fool our own souls and we will be left discomfited,
unhappy, and plagued by our consciences.[3]

A Dream Bigger than Oneself

In so many ways, Greek and Roman myths depict the struggle between ego and wisdom, an eternal struggle within which we are all forever caught. Golden Flame leadership has to do with choosing wisdom, and sacrificing one's own egoistic needs for something bigger than oneself. King Minos let his ego get the best of him and as a result, his legacy was forever sullied. Can you imagine giving up all that you have for the sake of a dream? Are you willing to subordinate your material desires to a dream of something bigger? Such is the essence of deep caring—of being a leader in service to something larger than oneself.

Each time that I was struck by a leader's force of character and the degree to which they live life without a safety net, I was subconsciously moved to examine my own answers to the questions above. I could feel at the tip of my awareness the disturbing realization that I was playing it safe, driven by egoistic desires while so many of the leaders I met on my journey were not. Someone once told me that the devil is the part of us that wants to believe we can live life fully and at the same time be safe and comfortable. As a result of my encounters, I can see more clearly that my life has been characterized by subtler and subtler ways of making calculated choices while seeking safety. Sure, I had started my own firm and helped nurture it to success. And I have often spoken the truth regardless of the consequences. But I have also lived a comfortable life, enamored with the external trappings that suggest success in the material world. In my heart of hearts, I know that my deeper purpose and the things I care about most have been tempered by careful calculation. I haven't been willing to risk it all for what I believe, and rarely do I put myself out there in ways that invite the potential for significant failure, for it is failure that I fear the most.

The Wolves Within

As I write these words, I can see ever more clearly that to find great leadership, I will have to search from within. I can't say yet whether I am yet a better leader than before having met these leaders on my journey, but I now know what it means to make courageous choices and what it means *not* to make them. And at this point I feel more ready to live my truth and my calling than ever before, whatever that may turn out to be.

Among Native Americans, there is a story they often tell around a fire that offers guidance to me in this regard. It is called "The Wolves Within."[4]

> *An old Grandfather said to his grandson, who came to him with anger at a friend who had done him an injustice...*
>
> *"Let me tell you a story. I, too, at times, have felt great hate for those who have taken so much, with no sorrow for what they do. But hate wears you down, and does not hurt your enemy. It's like taking poison and wishing your enemy would die.*
>
> *"I have struggled with these feelings many times. It is as if there are two wolves inside me; one is good and does no harm. He lives in harmony with all around him and does not take offense when no offense was intended. He will only fight when it is right to do so, and in the right way.*
>
> *"But...the other wolf... ah! The littlest thing will send him into a fit of temper. He fights everyone, all of the time, for no reason. He cannot think because his anger and hate are so great. It is helpless anger, for his anger will change nothing.*
>
> *"Sometimes it is hard to live with these two wolves inside me, for both of them try to dominate my spirit."*
>
> *The boy looked intently into his Grandfather's eyes and asked, "Which one wins, Grandfather?"*

The Grandfather smiled and quietly said, "The one I feed."

The question I keep asking myself is this: Do I feed the wolf of fear and greed and risk losing the life I've grown comfortable with, or do I feed my soul's desire and its care for the desires of others?

✧

Having explored the first two forces—a clear inner compass and a powerful anchor of values—that give rise to great leadership, we now come to our third and final force: a rock solid sense of self. This force has two primary components, each presented in the next two chapters: self-knowledge and self-compassion.

KEY POINTS IN CHAPTER 6

- Deep caring is fundamental to the lives of great leaders.

- They care for ideals, ideas, people, and humanity.

- They care for something beyond themselves.

- They have at least one thing that matters to them beyond all else.

- You cannot be a great leader and also play it safe.

CHAPTER 7

———— ◇ ————

A ROCK-SOLID SENSE OF SELF

*To be nobody-but-yourself—in a world
which is doing its best night and day, to
make you everybody else—means to fight
the hardest battle which any human being
can fight; and never stop fighting.*

—e. e. cummings

The rolling waves crash gently on the beach, but beyond the noise lies a deeper stillness. When I gaze at just the waves, the ocean seems turbulent, an endless undulation of unpredictable forces. One can easily get tossed and turned by its ferocity. But if I blur my eyes and observe the ocean from a broader perspective, its vastness and seemingly tranquil surface are enticing. I watch, I wait, and I listen. And in time, the sea begins to touch my soul. It gently rocks me from side to side, holding me by its outstretched arms. It calls for me to settle myself and quiet my internal chatter—to listen from a different place inside.

I know this place of calm, but don't visit it often. Instead, like most of us, I experience my daily waking life as an endless series of thoughts, decisions, and ruminations. The noise of my life engulfs me and I get lost in it. True leadership, I am learning, does not originate out of this noise, from the chatter in one's head. It comes from somewhere else.

In my life I have worked with many leaders. I have worked for them as an employee and I have worked with them as their guide and counsel. Many were excellent in their technical abilities, but few inspired me. Was it them or was it the lens through which I looked? More often than not, I looked for leadership in their deeds, expecting something that they couldn't deliver.

Now, on this journey, I'm discovering a new kind of leader and what effective leadership truly is. Have I begun to see them from a different place, with wider eyes and a more spacious heart? Is there something that these individuals are bringing forth that is unfamiliar to my previous experiences? Regardless of the reasons, these leaders seem different: More present. More clear. More human.

For example, Joseph Jaworski, CEO of Generon Consulting, said to me the moment we met, "So tell me about yourself." In the context of a meeting where I was to learn about him, he wanted to know about me, to make an authentic connection before we even started. And so began the revelation of how he became a leader, a process that led to an extraordinary connection between us that, in the end, brought me to tears for having reached a place that I rarely touch.

Robert Bobb, an experienced city manager who has worked in that role for many large cities, including Washington, D.C., the most politicized and therefore challenging city to be a city manager in I can imagine, is another example of someone with presence who spoke from the heart. When I began our interview by asking him about leadership, he instead started describing his grandmother, who grew up poor on a farm and yet rich in her heart. He reminisced about her unquenchable curiosity, and about the times they spent together reading. Mostly he read to her, for her reading abilities were minimal, and in those loving moments of shared discovery and wonder, Robert experienced a power in learning that helped shape the leader he is today. And by holding fast to a set of simple values including respect, excellence, honesty, and commitment, he stands as a rock of strength in the highly charged environment of city politics.

Scott Johnson of the Myelin Repair Foundation, an MS sufferer since age 20, converted his disability into a passion for research and innovation. Not only did he inspire others through his work but also through his strong convictions that led him to challenge the fundamental assumptions upon which medical scientific research is based.

With few exceptions, each of these leaders seemed completely comfortable in their body. They exuded inner confidence and inner knowing. They were, to use an oft-used word in psychology, centered. In contrast, I have seen so many leaders whose efforts to prove themselves and their worth resonated not from within but from their heads, from ego and ambition. When asked about leadership, they would talk about their own accomplishments.

> *With few exceptions, each of these leaders seemed completely at home in their body.*

The leaders I met deeply valued authentic relationships and were not afraid to admit their failings. Their demeanor was remarkably consistent as we discussed both their successes and failures, which they considered normal parts of their journey of life and learning. In speaking with them I was often reminded of Rudyard Kipling and his poem, *If*: "If you can meet Triumph and Disaster / and treat each of those two imposters just the same/ ... you will be a man, my son." To do so requires that you not only know yourself but that you accept yourself—that you are good with who you are. These two qualities make up what I call a "rock-solid sense of self." This chapter speaks to the first quality—self-knowledge, while the next chapter speaks to the second—self-compassion.

> *The leaders I met deeply valued authentic relationships and were not afraid to admit their failings.*

Knowing Oneself

On the surface, knowing oneself is often thought of as knowing one's strengths and weaknesses. Certainly the many books out there about personality type and core competencies are a testament to this inclination. Indeed, the leaders I met would likely argue that knowing their strengths and weaknesses *is* a key to their success. Being at peace with their personal limitations creates an opening for better leadership. For example, they can more confidently delegate certain responsibilities to those who have abilities that they don't have. Chris Chavez, CEO of Advanced Neuromodulation Systems, stressed, "You have to surround yourself with people who complement you and who balance you and ... who will tell you what you *need* to know, not what you *want* to know."

But knowing oneself goes much deeper than knowing one's strengths and weaknesses. It has to do with knowing one's own essential nature and being true to that nature. It has to do with seeing the deeper patterns that course through one's life—patterns that define us as unique and distinct. In a sense, each of us broke the mold when we were born. We express ourselves uniquely through our language, our art, and our personality, and especially in those rich moments where we break all convention and surrender to our inspirations.

I've been coaching a leader for a while now who is troubled by the fact that he doesn't like to plan. He prefers spontaneity and freedom. At the same time, he values reliability and knows that for his company to become great, it needs a strong direction and specific goals. In his struggle to reconcile these opposing forces, he confided in me that he felt he was letting his team down, that he wasn't keeping his commitments and failing to be a good role model. I felt that a deeper pattern had to be considered:

making too many specific promises simply didn't fit his native tendencies. I suggested that he acknowledge to his team that creative thinking and building community are more to his strengths, but that consistency and reliability are vital to the company's success and need attention. Admitting such truths would model a leader who is true to himself while taking the pressure off to be someone he wasn't. It would also free him up to invite others to step up and take on more responsibility.

My client was facing a common disconnect between what naturally drives a person and obeisance to other values. The ability to mediate between these two forces is one of the marks of exceptional leadership. Unfortunately, many respond to this conflict by giving in to the "should" game: We should do this but not that. The casualty of this game is usually the soul's deeper calling—and we wonder why we don't feel fulfilled. There are those cases when one's values and soul's desire meet in blissful alignment and integration, but that's not usually the case. Societal pressures, parental expectations, and our company's needs more often call to us to be someone we are not.

Knowing who one is—and who one is *not*—is extraordinarily challenging in this day and age. From his nineteenth-century vantage point, Ralph Waldo Emerson echoed similar words as that of e.e. cummings (quoted at the beginning of this chapter) when he said, "To be yourself in a world that is constantly trying to make you something else is the greatest accomplishment." From parents, school, and peers, ideas were drummed into our heads about right behavior and how to measure success. And in the media, we are deluged with images of celebrities and lifestyles that promise some semblance of happiness. And yet, as a culture, we are further from happiness than ever before, and we are certainly far from healthy. According to ongoing research by the Kaiser Family Foundation, for example, spending in the U.S. for prescription drugs increased more than five-fold from 1990 to 2006, while sales of antidepressants have nearly tripled since 1997.[1]

Perhaps the chase for success as defined by something outside of us is the actual cause of our dis-ease—and of our inability to be in touch with our core self. A growing number of psychologists are now asserting exactly that. For example, Thomas Moore and James Hillman have written eloquently about how our psychological and emotional ailments have less to do with our upbringing than with how we have cut ourselves off from our essential soul nature—a notion we will examine in more detail later in the book. Observing how standout leaders present themselves as fully engaged and guided by an inner compass gives us a taste for what is possible.

To begin, let's look at the multiple layers of what it means to be human. At the deepest level of who we are exists the *core self*—the innate resonance of our soul. At this core lies stillness, an inner peace, a knowing that all that we are is connected to everything else. When we are at peace with ourselves in this way, without a need to *become* something, we begin to connect with our soul's deepest yearnings. When we live from within and express these desires, we feel alive and full, and at one with (rather than threatened by) others and their success. We have all experienced this feeling at one time or another, however fleeting it may have been. Most of the world's great religious and spiritual traditions recognize this ultimate but elusive state of grace and have practices designed to achieve it. Although most of us are strangers to our core self and our soul's calling (at least most of the time), the experience of the core self is universal—that is, it crosses all boundaries of religion, culture, and worldview—and it is universally valued among those who have experienced it. While the soul's calling may be different in each of us, we all share the phenomenon of its presence.

Figure 7-1: The First Layer of Human Being

At the next layer we find our *personality*. Personality comes from the root word "persona," which was the word for "mask" in Greek drama.

So the personality can be understood as the mask that we show to the world. Being a mask, it is not as deep as the core self, and in most of us it tends to disguise the existence of the core self. It is what we consciously or unconsciously choose to show the world, and it is what the world sees or chooses to see—or, more specifically, what the world *infers* from what it sees.

To understand the concept of personality, imagine that you had the opportunity to observe someone and record all of his or her behavior, moment by moment. Now imagine that you could categorize these types of behavior like voice inflection, facial expressions, bodily movements, and speech. Now attempt to see patterns or similarities among these behaviors. Finally, imagine that you were to codify these patterns and compare them to the patterns displayed by others. This codification is, in effect, your map of a personality. This process, directly or intuitively, is what psychologists have been doing ever since Aristotle formed the first personality taxonomy more than two thousand years ago.

Figure 7-2: The Second Layer of Human Being

There are many systems for understanding differences in personality. Among the more popular is the Myers-Briggs Type Indicator, which is largely derived from Carl Jung's original observations about differences among people. The Enneagram of Personality is another such typology and one that I prefer, for it offers a deeper understanding of the patterns that cause the formation of our personalities. Originating as early as 2500 BC as a complex nine-point schema of esoteric knowledge, it was introduced to the modern world by the mystic G.I. Gurdjieff in the 1930s. Several decades later, philosopher Oscar Ichazo (director of the Arica Institute) applied his own theories to the Enneagram, and psychiatrist Claudio Naranjo then further refined the model.[2] Today there are numerous interpretations and applications of the Enneagram typology.

While there are differences among personality typologies, they have a number of common assumptions. Central among them is that our personality represents ingrained patterns of behavior that have become a part of us. While individual behaviors will vary, the patterns often remain unchanged throughout adult life. Moreover, there is no inherent goodness or badness among personalities. There are, of course, unhealthy *expressions* of personality. For example, the personality of World War II hero General MacArthur—that of a *driver, controller,* or *commander* in many personality taxonomies—is not inherently problematic. Witness the many effective military as well as civilian leaders who have a similarly strong and controlling personality. The problem with MacArthur was the extreme way in which he expressed this personality in the form of excessive narcissism. Ultimately, his uncontrollable desire to be the center of attention proved to be his Achilles' heel, perhaps preventing him from being acknowledged as among the great military leaders of all time.

By adulthood, our personality is deeply etched into our psyches. Some have argued that it is genetically baked into our personhood and should not be altered, for to do so would alter our "natural" state, causing angst, discomfort, and disease. Most psychologists believe that, to be healthy at the level of personality, it is better to understand and accept one's personality than to try to change it. That doesn't mean that our personality is rigid and can only be expressed in a certain way. Rather, most experts say, we can learn fluidity and flexibility and should strive to express our personality in more healthy and mature ways. Because it is more on the surface of our humanness, it is far easier to mold or evolve our personality than it is to change our core self.

At the outermost layer of human experience lies our *behavior*—the daily actions, decisions, and choices we make (see Figure 7-3). Naturally, there are an infinite variety of behaviors one can exhibit, and they change, moment by moment.

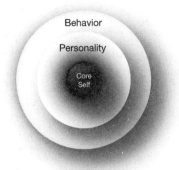

Figure 7-3: The Three Layers of Human Being

While there are endless variations in our behaviors, they do tend to form patterns because our behavior is influenced by our personality and by the qualities and expression of our core self. There is, in fact, a causal relationship among these layers of human beingness. Inner affects outer far more than the other way around (see Figure 7-4).

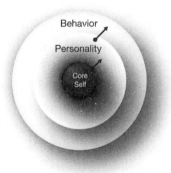

Figure 7-4: The Relationship Between Layers of Being

The further we get from the center, the more variety we see among human beings. Perhaps an analogy will be helpful. Our core self is much like the deepest part of the ocean—relatively still, quiet, and hardly moving. Further up from the ocean floor there begins to be more movement as deep currents undulate and roll—motion can be felt. Yet compared to the surface, it is still a calmer and more stable place. As currents from below break the ocean's surface, the motion becomes constant, sometimes turbulent and other times less so but ever moving. It is visible to the naked eye but you don't see the churning below. In the same way, our behaviors are visible to others. All we can actually *see* in another individual is their behavior; we then infer what lies below (Figure 7-5).

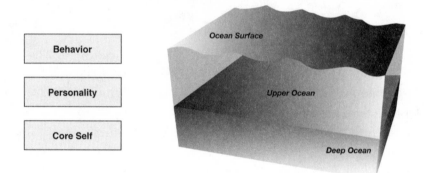

Figure 7-5: The Ocean of Self

Our connection—or *lack* of connection—to our essence or core self determines our personality and behavior. When our core self is denied or ignored, we cut ourselves off from that which we most truly are, and our ability to relate to others and to the world suffers. We then become vulnerable to influences from outside of ourselves. To the extent that we chase someone else's definition of success, for example, we live a life that is not our own. In our unacknowledged despair and lack of purpose, we numb ourselves with food or drink, TV or video games, the newspaper or the Internet, gossip or movies. The motivations for these actions are so automatic and unconscious that we're hardly aware of numbing ourselves in the first place—at least not until the negative consequences of our actions (or the concerns of our friends or our family) force us to wake up. Until we know and embrace who we are and let go of who we aren't, we can never be happy or fulfilled.

> *Until we know and embrace who we are and let go of who we aren't, we can never be happy or fulfilled.*

What does it look like to operate from your inner essence? Numerous examples have been presented in this book, but one of the most personally inspiring was Kartar Singh Khalsa, the CEO of Golden Temple Foods. Golden Temple is the largest supplier of bulk granola in the health foods industry and maker of the popular Yogi Tea. Kartar, a deeply spiritual man, runs his company on the value of inner peace. An American by heritage, he is also a Sikh, as are most of the executives on his leadership team.

The principal belief of Sikhism is faith in *Vahiguru*—the Universal God experienced and seen as a universal, ever-present force. The followers of Sikhism devote their lives to self-understanding, connection to all, and an abiding commitment to spiritual awakening. Sikhs can be seen throughout the world wearing their trademark white turbans and white robes, signifying their vow to a pure life.

Guided by the principles and beliefs of Sikhism as interpreted by his spiritual leader Harbhajan Singh Yogi, Kartar leads by example. He does it with ease, candor, and ongoing self-inquiry. I was impressed not only by his devotion but also by a powerful sense of who he is and the humility and grace with which he expressed it. He is clearly in contact with his essence, his core self. When discussing some of the changes he was guiding his company toward, he spoke about the challenges of leadership and what it required:

> *You have to tap into your own spirit, and that's there in everybody. You know inside yourself what you should be doing. If you choose to listen to that and make changes, which may be very hard changes, you are making changes that are authentic to your own self, and then true leadership naturally comes out.*

I had the privilege of spending a day with Kartar's leadership team, and was deeply impressed with how devoted they are and how they keep their spiritual tenets at the center of their work. For them, work isn't separate from spirit but emanates from it. How many companies do you know of that are guided by a spiritual source? It's an unusual model, and in the case of Golden Temple Foods, has led to consistently outstanding results.

> *With few exceptions, each of these leaders seemed completely at home in their body.*

Self-discovery is both a *journey* and a *process,* and you can't expect it to happen overnight. It requires a great deal of soul-searching and deep psychological work. The backgrounds and experiences of those I interviewed were varied, but each had a rock-solid sense of who they were and felt good about who they had become. And while no single event or experience was common to their shared commitment to self-learning, many referred to childhood experiences that influenced their leadership journey.

One such individual was Mary Taverna. When I interviewed her, she was about to retire as president and CEO of Hospice of Marin (since renamed Hospice by the Bay) after a long and fruitful stewardship of the organization. Mary, along with others, was instrumental in bringing the hospice movement to the U.S. in the early 1970s (see Chapter 6). When she was exposed to the idea as a young nurse, the idea of a community of family and health care providers shepherding the dying through that precarious passage was almost unheard of here. Mary saw the potency of such a movement and applied her heart and soul to the challenge of bringing it to the U.S.

In order to accomplish her goal, she had to learn the legal and political intricacies of the existing health care system. Undaunted by repeated trial and error, she learned a lot, persevered, and, along with others, finally succeeded. When I asked her what it took to carry her through, she said, "I believed that if I kept accepting the challenge, embracing the challenge, and learning, that I could go as far as I wanted in this field. I had great belief; I had great passion."

That belief was palpable when I met Mary. When I asked her about the source of that belief, she spoke passionately about her family:

> My grandmother was self-sufficient and comfortable with her life as a seamstress, but she had a belief that I could do just about anything. I also had a father who went from being a boy on a ranch to achieving professional excellence without ever finishing high school. Those two role models planted seeds in me that I could do and be whatever I wanted. I tell my staff that they can do anything if they believe in themselves and find the right people to help them get there.

The sureness of Mary's voice, the confidence in her words, and the openness with which she explored deep questions of self-revelation spoke not only to her rock-solid sense of self but transported me to that same place within myself. I had this experience over and over again in my meetings with these leaders. Just being in their presence both inspired me and reminded me of my essential core.

Ego versus Wisdom

Carl Jung, the great Swiss psychiatrist, laid down the gauntlet for self-knowledge when he said,

> Nowhere are we closer to the sublime secret of all origination than in the recognition of our own selves, whom we always think we know already. Yet we know

the immensities of space better than we know our own
depths, where—even though we do not understand it—
we can listen directly to the throb of creation itself.[3]

Centuries before Jung, similar sentiments were expressed. Etched into the stonewalls of Apollo's temple at Delphi are the words, "Know thyself." Socrates, too, saw inner knowledge as the key to a whole and meaningful life. Siddhartha Gautama (the Buddha) expressed it in his aphorism: right attitude, skillful means. Each is calling for the same thing: *Seek inner knowledge first.*

Great leaders demonstrate outward effectiveness because they are coming from and behaving consistent with the resonance of their core self. The most important aspect of their self-knowledge has to do with understanding the distinction between operating from ego and from inner wisdom. When leaders are at their best, they put their ego aside and let wisdom be their guide.

For the sake of simplicity and clarity, I use the term "ego" in a way that is derived from Buddhism and much of Eastern philosophy: a part of "the self" that tries to protects us, and in particular our view of the world. Buddhists contend that we form beliefs about the world and the people in it, and that from these beliefs we form judgments, deciding what we like and don't like through the subjective lens of this judgmental ego. Interpreting the world in this way helps us feel safe by validating our perspective and reinforcing a belief that we are right and others are wrong.

Wisdom, on the other hand, is the ability to see the world and take action from a place of peace, certainty, compassion, and non-attachment to outcome. All wisdom teachings, from Zen Buddhism to Sufism to the Toltec tradition, share the idea that inner peace and outer effectiveness go hand in hand. It is inner peace that ushers in a deeper sense of knowing. This kind of knowing is in direct contrast with the "shallow knowing" that our Western society tends to value, which primarily consists of acquiring facts and information.

When I view the world from ego, I see it through a distorted lens driven by my needs and my fears. When I engage the world from the viewpoint

> *All wisdom teachings share the idea that inner peace and outer effectiveness go hand in hand.*

of my inner wisdom, there is no need to manipulate or hide or "spin" my experience, and I am able to see and act with more clarity.

Accessing Core Knowledge

The journey toward remarkable leadership is a journey of self-knowledge that has no end. The more one is aware of one's motivations, needs, and drives—rather than simply acting on autopilot—the more effective he or she becomes. Not surprisingly, nearly all of the leaders I interviewed valued this journey tremendously, perhaps more than anything else in their lives. Judith Rogala put it well when she said, "My definition of great leadership is knowing who you are and what you believe—what your core values are; talking about it within the organization; exposing yourself, if you will; and being true to those values. You can't trust others until you trust yourself. Such trust can only come from self-knowledge."

> *The journey toward remarkable leadership is a journey of self-knowledge that has no end.*

Will Rosensweig is a wonderful example of someone who has achieved great leadership after deep self-reflection. Will was co-founder and then CEO of The Republic of Tea, the award-winning specialty tea company that is often credited with creating the premium tea category in the United States. More than the tea itself, the quality of the company's culture spoke volumes about the quality of Will as a leader. It's a highly progressive culture committed to social responsibility and a healthy lifestyle. Among other things, The Republic of Tea employees have extraordinary freedom to make choices that benefit the good of the company—including the freedom to make up their own job titles—and feel a powerful sense of personal accountability.

Will believes that people as well as organizations benefit when *consciousness*—simply put, awareness of self and one's impact on others—is placed at the center of all action. His university lectures on the subject of becoming an entrepreneur, along with his gentle, straightforward, and unassuming demeanor, glow with his passionate call to living a healthy life and contributing to a healthy planet. Will has little desire to be in the public eye. As he said to me, there are "so many leaders" who seem to aspire to become "high-profile celebrities" in which "they have a book, they have a movie, or they use their company for personal means and ends. That sort of leadership is something I've always been a bit reluctant about."

Instead of wanting the limelight, Will has a huge desire to make a difference. Like so many of the leaders I met, his life is purposeful. As I sat with him on a bench overlooking San Francisco Bay, he spoke calmly and with conviction about his life and business philosophy—and particularly about his passion for gardening. For him, gardening is both a path of awakening and a metaphor for life. "Growing a culture, like a garden, takes time," he reflected. "It requires care and feeding."

Now in his fifties, Will speaks about giving to others. He is a living example of the power of *generativity*, a term coined by the late developmental psychologist Erik Erikson. In his research and writing, Erikson described what he believed to be the natural and healthy phases of a person's life. He is best known for exploring, and actually naming, the phenomenon of the mid-life crisis. His work was the precursor to Gail Sheehy's popular book *Passages* and, before her, Harry Levinson's book *Seasons of a Man's Life.* In Erikson's teachings and those that followed, he believed that becoming truly satisfied in the latter part of one's life has less to do with being productive and more to do with passing our gifts on to others. Will and many of the leaders I met had an awareness that their mission in life was ultimately to inspire others. With this intention in mind, Will founded Great Spirit Ventures after leaving The Republic of Tea, and then co-founded and led Brand New Brands. Recently, he has merged these two efforts into one—Physic Ventures. With his new initiative, he continues to carry on his devotion to help seed a new generation of health-minded consumers and entrepreneurs, and feels that his greatest gifts of teaching have come alive in this work. What inspired me the most about Will, though, was his image of leadership as an ultimately vulnerable act:

> *I think that extraordinary leadership is the ability and willingness to make oneself vulnerable in a power structure that traditionally doesn't have that kind of vulnerability. To be able to sit with somebody and say, 'I could be wrong about this. I'm willing to be wrong, and I have been wrong, and if that shakes your boat then let's have the conversation.'*

In Will's world, full openness is absolutely integral to true leadership. Such openness requires a solid sense of self. I find it more than curious that the leaders who are *least* secure are the ones we perceive as most arrogant and impenetrable. The ones who are *most* secure in who they are come across as the most vulnerable. In a world where too many leaders equate might with right and are prone to believing that they must know the answer or they don't deserve to lead, such vulnerability appears as weakness. In the world of many of the leaders I met, the opposite is true. They envision a world where leaders don't play parent while employees are forced into the role of children. Instead, they desire a world where everyone steps up as adult leaders. In such a world, vulnerability and the capacity to engage others in truthful and open conversation is crucial to a deeper and more sustainable level of success. Great leaders bring forth honesty in *everyone*, not just in themselves.

> *The leaders who are* least *secure are*
> *the ones we perceive as most*
> *arrogant and impenetrable. The ones*
> *who are* most *secure in who they are*
> *come across as the most vulnerable.*

When someone is solid in his or her sense of self, speaking one's inner truth comes easily and often. At the same time, there is plenty of room for the views and truths of others. There is plenty of room to admit mistakes, for they are just a natural part of life—nothing to be hidden and certainly not worthy of shame. And to have a rock-solid sense of self is *not* to always have the answer, but to trust and feel comfortable with an interactive process in which answers can be discovered creatively and collaboratively, where everyone is part of the solution.

KEY POINTS IN CHAPTER 7
- A rock solid sense of self includes two qualities: deeply knowing oneself and being good with oneself.

- As a result of these qualities, great leaders are comfortable in their own skin.

- It is from the core of oneself that lays a sense of ease and stillness.

- Knowing oneself takes time—reflection and learning, and a willingness to penetrate the veneer of one's defenses.

- Acting from true wisdom comes from self-knowledge.

CHAPTER 8

---------- ◇ ----------

THE POWER OF SELF-COMPASSION

*It is ironic but very true that we are often
the last ones in the world to be able to see
and acknowledge our own gifts.*

—e. e. cummings

K nowing oneself is the first half of the equation for having a rock-solid sense of self. Being good with that self—accepting who you are with grace and confidence and then living from that acceptance—is the second and equally important half. A rock-solid sense of self emanates from the feeling of inner peace that comes from being completely at ease with one's essential nature. Such people are seen as centered, self–possessed, and confident in the truest sense. Their calm bearing, and the remarkable ease with which they express that, are contagious. Psychologists know this all too well. They spend most of their professional lives helping others find a sense of well-being and self-esteem. When you have high self-esteem, you naturally follow your own inner compass. You trust yourself, and others are more comfortable trusting you. "When you listen to your inner voice telling you what to think, say, and do," said Jerry Jampolsky, founder of the Center for Attitudinal Healing, "you become a powerful magnet for others who say, 'Hey, I want some of that inner peace too.'"

Maslow's View of Self-Esteem

Perhaps more than anyone in the past half-century, Abraham Maslow articulated the features of which I speak. Throughout his adult life, Maslow was drawn to and investigated the experience of extraordinary well-being. He was less interested in what causes psychological disease than in what gives rise to psychological health. In his exploration, Maslow postulated that our needs could be organized in a functional hierarchy, where one's lower-rung needs must be met before the next level of needs can be attended to.

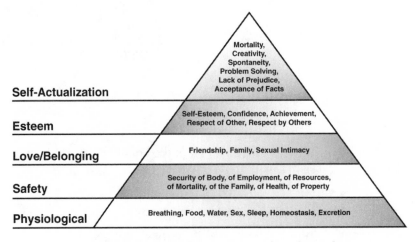

Figure 8-1: Maslow's Hierarchy of Needs

While his hierarchy of needs is what made him famous, it was his unbridled fascination with the high states of psychological health that was his signature inspiration, the beginning point of which is self-esteem. Maslow, as have many others, defined self-esteem as self-respect or self-valuing. Beyond self-esteem are the highest reaches of human nature—what he called the *self-actualized* person. He defined self-actualization as the *instinctual* need of humans to make the most of their unique abilities and to strive to be the best they can be. Maslow believed that arriving at full self-actualization, while rare, is an expression of our human potential, an *"intrinsic growth of what is already in the organism, or more accurately, of what is the organism itself."*[1]

My own experience of the leaders I met on my journey is that most of them had achieved or were close to achieving a level of self-actualization. They seemed at ease in their body, present in the moment, fluid and flexible, and surprisingly humble—the kind of humility borne not from meekness but from knowing that life is a journey of learning that never ends. And because these people weren't pretentious and had no need to prove themselves, I found myself immediately comfortable in their presence because they acknowledged my value not as a professional but as a fellow human being.

> *My own experience of the leaders*
> *I met on my journey is that most*
> *of them had achieved or were close to*
> *achieving a level of self-actualization.*

Sometimes I can feel the same sense of ease and solidity in myself, and other times I am shaken. The knowledge that I am still shaky as a leader came to sharp relief recently when giving a talk, along with two of my colleagues, before 100 professionals at a conference on the current state of the field of organizational development (OD).

In our respective presentations, the three of us challenged OD professionals to look hard at how they practice their profession. We discussed some of the underlying assumptions that have led many OD consultants to be marginalized or dismissed as minimally relevant by the leaders of organizations and companies. We soared and struggled through a rigorous exploration of the ills that plague the profession and the opportunities that lay ahead. As primary facilitator of the experience, I felt satisfied that my colleagues and I had accomplished what we set out to do. And, as expected, the responses were passionate and mixed; our boldness sparked plenty of dialogue and exchange, as well as some anger and frustration. After all, we were questioning some of the ways that people conduct themselves as consultants and the assumptions that underlie that conduct.

Many said it was a great experience and were grateful that we challenged our profession to step up. Some said that they wished we had given clearer answers. A few were discouraged and even outraged by our presentation. What surprised and troubled me, however, was a small group of women who expressed their outrage quite publicly. Apparently they took a comment I made about the need for more "King energy" as sexist, and it clearly pushed some buttons. One woman said I should have used the more gender-neutral term "regal." I replied that I was referring to the archetypical notion of king energy in relationship to a male consultant I knew who seemed to embody such energy quite effectively. Since he was a man, I explained, referring to "King" seemed natural. She was not persuaded, and called my behavior chauvinistic. Being a person deeply committed to inclusiveness, the charge cut deep, not because it seemed true but because it seemed so untrue and was expressed so publicly.

For days the meeting gnawed at me, so much so I felt compelled to reach out to women I knew who were at the conference to get their feedback. To a person they said they did not experience me as sexist at all, though they understood how the few outraged others could have misinterpreted my comments that way. Instead, they saw me as strong, direct, and willing to take an unpopular stand and speak my truth.

In trying to sort all this out, I found most troubling my emotional reaction to the accusations, and linked it back to leadership. In observing my inner dialogue about the event, I realized how much I wanted everyone in the audience to like and respect me. From the many who did, I felt soothed by their encouragement. From the few who didn't, I felt misunderstood, hurt, and even angry. "They just don't get me," my inner child kept saying. "How dare they!" roared my inner protective parent. "I've got to fix this," said my inner strategist, who wanted to be sure that my reputation stayed intact. In the spirit of a technique called voice dialogue,[1] I came to see these voices as natural parts of me, voices that most of us have. Who wouldn't rather be liked and respected than dismissed and ignored?

Caught in my own inner chatter, I telephoned one of my co-presenters, a trusted advisor, to share and process my feelings. "Congratulations," he said, "I was delighted with the session. You and I stood up and spoke our truth. We were challenging them and ruffled some feathers. How could we have expected otherwise? After all, we were telling them that they aren't nearly as effective as they could be. And that claim of sexism was unfounded in my view. If you're going to be a leader, you've got to be willing to take the heat. I say let it go."

His words helped me to accept that what happened was inevitable, both the support and the disdain, and that it couldn't be any other way. In the land of leadership, universal support isn't possible. I then remembered what I had helped teach others: That great leadership starts with following one's own inner compass, unencumbered by concerns of being liked or disliked.

The incident had many lessons for me and helped me realize that I still have further to go in my journey, for those inner voices of hurt and need rose all too quickly to the surface. The point is not to suppress them—there will always be tender parts of us that arise from time to time—but to keep them from crowding out the deeper self that knows its truth and is willing to speak it. That's why the journey of becoming a great leader didn't happen overnight for the leaders I met; it emerged over time, the fruits of a life-long commitment to discovering who they are at their core. While it's impossible to reduce such a journey into a one-size-fits-all formula, *self-compassion* seems to be the universal attribute at the root of their experience.

Honoring the Self

All great leaders know that the journey of learning and self-discovery is a never-ending process of self-compassion. This is not the same thing as having a positive judgment of yourself. True self-compassion involves insight, not judgment. The more you judge yourself, the harder it is to see yourself. The harder it is to see yourself, the less you know. And the less you know about what makes you tick, the more your actions are driven by psychological needs and distortions than from wisdom that is grounded in truth.

Self-compassion means that you recognize all of the forces inside of yourself—dark and light, mercurial and persistent, petulant and powerful, foolish and wise—as natural parts of you. You aren't denying these forces, condemning them, or judging them as good or bad. Instead, you are accepting them for what they are in a spirit of understanding and applying that recognition in ways that serve all people, including yourself.

Self-compassion is more than self-acceptance—a term that has been in vogue in the world of psychology for a long time. To accept is not enough. Self-compassion invokes an image of self-care that can lead to ease and grace. When someone is compassionate with oneself, their natural response to feedback or criticism is curiosity and self–reflection— not the self-judgment, self-remorse, or defensiveness that more often than not gets triggered. This quality of self-compassion opens a person to learning about themselves and their impact on others. With self-compassion, the sting associated with admitting mistakes is gone—everything becomes an opportunity for personal growth.

Leaders who are guided by self-compassion naturally accept others as they are, without judgment, which enables them to act more wisely. They talk not in terms of absolute goodness or badness but in terms of what works given the needs of a particular situation and the limitations or strengths of a given individual, and this is always a process of discovery.

> *Leaders who are guided by self-compassion naturally accept others as they are, without judgment.*

While, as a group, the leaders I met were much more self-aware and open than most people I know, some had moments of self-aggrandizement or self-delusion. The ego has an enormous ability to "strut its stuff," and these leaders, like the rest of us, were not immune to its power. And yet with rare exception they noticed the moments when this was happening and adjusted back into a more thoughtful and relational manner—without judging themselves. This is important, for it is the act of self-judgment that helps to feed and sustain the ego. As soon as we judge something about ourselves as "wrong," we either reflexively condemn it (or condemn ourselves) or deny it exists because we don't want to see ourselves as "bad." In either case, the ego effectively disowns it and it tends to go underground, unavailable to our conscious awareness. This is what Carl Jung meant when he referred to the *shadow* parts of ourselves.

Unfortunately, these shadow parts end up shaping our lives, whether we're consciously aware of it or not. For example, witness those who fervently deny that they have "control issues" as they try to control others or rigidly refuse to conform to anybody or anything else. This denial reflects an unmet recognition of their need not be controlled. In so doing, they never have to admit that such a part exists and thus they never have to deal with it—leaving that to those who are negatively affected by their behavior.

Even in the best of leaders these shadow parts sometimes showed up, reminding me that they were still human. One leader, for example, expressed his strong belief that a leader should be direct and honest with others. "A good leader," he told me, "earns respect by delivering tough messages. If someone does something wrong, I'll sit him or her down and tell the truth," Yet I am told by people who know him well that this very same leader is notoriously hesitant to speak difficult truths. His effectiveness as a leader, they say, is due more to his compassion than his ability to confront others.

Did he believe he was being honest or was he stating something that wasn't true but that perhaps he thought made him look more effective? It's hard to know. What I do know is that the ability to admit difficult truths about oneself is at the heart of self-acceptance. Great leaders, like the rest of us, have their blind spots and areas where further growth and learning is needed.

Knowing a bit about his pattern, I offered the leader feedback, saying that others might be puzzled by his views about himself as being a tough leader compared to his actual behavior. In contrast to other leaders who might be affronted by such feedback, he was the opposite. He smiled and chuckled and said that maybe he was over-selling himself and that it was indeed hard for him to confront others. At the same time, he believed it was a crucial part of his learning edge. In short, instead of being defensive, he was wonderfully curious and open.

Such is the *sine qua non* of great leadership: It's not about perfection but about compassionately accepting all of whom one is, making room for the strengths as well as the weaknesses. Allowing those shadow parts in by acknowledging their existence gives us the capacity to influence them. When we begin to see more clearly who we are, without judgment, we begin to self-integrate and become more whole. From that place the decisions we make will have a more positive and powerful impact on any situation.

A Deeper Sense of Integrity

The word *integrity* has many meanings. To some, it's synonymous with honesty—doing what you say you will do, telling the truth (or not trying to spin the truth), saying what you believe, not cheating people, and being open to whatever is real in your life and circumstances. It speaks of living consistently with one's values. But to me, the term *integrity* also has a much deeper meaning. It has to do with the notion of being *integrated*. When my words and my deeds are aligned, I am integrated. When I live consistent with my own code, I am integrated. When I follow my own muse, living from my soul, I am integrated. This richer view of integrity means that the life I live is consistent with who I am at my core. To live with integrity therefore requires that I know my deepest self—that I dare to peel back the layers and find the stirrings that live within.

"I want to get the word out to the world that it's okay to be who you are," said Judith Rogala, who has run numerous companies throughout her career. "This is crucial for people throughout the entire organization, not just the CEO. To be true to yourself is the key to leadership and, more importantly, the key to a successful life."

> *To live with integrity therefore*
> *requires that I know my*
> *deepest self.*

I recently experienced a powerful example of the potency of true integrity—of having a rock-solid sense of self and self-compassion—and the all-too-familiar dysfunctional work environments that result when leaders lack these qualities.

One of my clients is a large division of a major U.S. government agency. Many of the executives there have hired me over the years to help their business units get strategically aligned and improve their execution capability. One of the biggest issues this particular division faced was dealing with a leader (we'll call him Steve) who had the reputation of being a typical government bureaucrat. Steve, a highly political and power-oriented player, liked to manipulate people, make capricious decisions, and ask others for input (having once learned in a workshop that good leaders do this so that people feel listened to) without any intention to do anything other than what he'd already decided to do. To make matters worse, he had no clear strategy for the division.

When I met Steve to discuss some of the challenges the division was having, he seemed friendly enough, although also quite nervous. He fidgeted in his chair, talked nonstop about all the wonderful things he had done in his career, and told me of his marvelous plans for the division, which sounded more like a wish list than anything resembling a well-thought-out strategy. When I mentioned some of the difficulties that people were having in the division and with him, he quickly blamed others and became extremely defensive. In short, Steve was a highly insecure leader, and it soon became clear that as long as he was at the helm, this division was destined for mediocre performance.

And so the division bumbled along as the managers reporting to Steve did their best to provide solid leadership to their particular constituencies in spite of getting little of the same from Steve. Finally, due to a series of circumstances, Steve was let go, replaced by someone we'll call Kevin. In contrast to Steve's tendency toward self-aggrandizement, Kevin began his tenure by speaking clearly about his own inexperience and need for support. Although relatively young, he was mature beyond his years. He was able to quickly elicit the support of the other executives and began to chart a shared strategy for success. In a state of wonder and appreciation, one of the executives who worked with Kevin said, "In the face of my wanting to make a risky but important reorganization of my unit, Kevin's response was, 'I support you. You make the call.' I never felt that from Steve."

Here it's important to differentiate between a rock-solid sense of self and a "rock-solid" sense of one's agenda or plan as a leader. Clearly, the first does not necessarily imply the second, as Kevin's case shows. He came into his position fully acknowledging his dependence on the support of others. In fact, if one has a rock-solid sense of self, as Kevin clearly does, it means one is able to comfortably live with uncertainty and to fully recognize that we live in a state of interdependence, where all the parts affect each other as well as the whole. And so given what I know of the relationship between a rock-solid sense of self and leadership success, I predict that this particular division will do just fine and spend our tax dollars with greater thoughtfulness and care.

15,000 Miracles

I believe that this exploration of self-compassion warrants a return to Mimi Silbert, the founder, president, and CEO of Delancey Street Foundation, who I introduced earlier in the book. Among all the leaders I met, she's the one I would nominate as the poster child for knowing, accepting, and believing in oneself. Defying all conventional limitations, Mimi seems to have integrated an extraordinary vision and lofty ideals with a down-to-earth respect for reality while charting a new path in her industry. She's a frame-breaker, someone who has "boldly gone where no one has gone before." She embodies all of the qualities of remarkable leadership discussed so far, with an especially solid sense of self. Her story needs to be shouted from the rooftops.

Without any map to guide her but with moxie, a powerful belief in herself, and an abiding appreciation for the family environment she grew up in, Mimi started Delancey Street as a way of putting troubled souls back into society so that they are not only able to survive and function but to thrive in body and spirit. Among the people who have become residents of her organization are felons, addicts, drug dealers, and gang leaders. She operates with a deep belief that all of them can change if given the right kind of conditions and a lot of love. Her residential home and the foundation's multiple businesses (staffed solely by the residents) are based on two suppositions which Mimi seems to know instinctively: first, if you just give people a handout, it might temporarily help them but won't produce a fundamental change; and second, if you provide a healthy family-like environment (which most of them never had), that structure and nurturing will help cause a shift in thinking. The result of her efforts: a sociological and business miracle.

Mimi began Delancey Street in 1971 with a thousand dollars and a desire to help others in distress, and the social system she created has reformed troubled souls with amazing consistency. Nearly four decades after its inception, Delancey Street, named after the section of New York where immigrants assembled more than a century ago, is now considered one of the nation's leading self-help residential education centers for the underclass in need. It has turned around the lives of over 15,000 people.

Mimi's Vision and Purpose

After missing her on my initial visit to Delancey, I ultimately had the pleasure of spending three hours with Mimi at her restaurant, and was deeply moved by her enthusiasm for her work and her appreciation for the gift of life. I was especially impressed by her humanity and lack of pretense. During our time together, three things became clear: she is powerfully determined to make a difference; she cares deeply about the people who work for her; and her work is, in the deepest sense I can imagine, a labor of love.

Mimi's model for working with society's outliers is, by its very nature, a frame-breaking model. Our country and many others in the Western world operate within a dysfunctional paradigm about "criminals" or those who are "troubled" that, in most respects, is designed to keep them that way. We shame them. We treat them with scorn and judgment. We do little to change the conditions that helped to create them. The socio-political system for dealing with these people can be broken down into two fundamental and opposing (but similarly ineffectual) views or frames. The conservative view emphasizes punishment and self-responsibility over compassion and acknowledgment of systemic problems; the liberal view stresses compassion and systemic problems over justice and personal responsibility.

At one extreme, the most tough-minded conservatives say that society owes nothing to the underprivileged except "opportunity"—which simply means they have a right to lift themselves up by their own bootstraps. Such a view ignores all the ways that one's own assumptions of what is possible are themselves the products of upbringing and life experience, or that the system itself may be rigged against them. The liberal view, in contrast, claims that people are impoverished due to the social system in which they grew up; therefore, they are not to blame and we should help them. We do this in the form of welfare and similar means that tend to foster dependency and can prolong destructive behaviors.

Both of these perspectives have some grain of truth in Mimi's view. It is what she calls mutual restitution. The convicts owe society to become the new best version of themselves—to give back and to give to others as opposed to take from others. And society owes them the open doors—to need the underclass and take full advantage of their true talents and new skills.

Both perspectives however, ignore some very important truths that Mimi has built into her vision. Yes, she acknowledges, the environment has a lot to do with how people turn out, and her organization responds to that by creating an atmosphere that leads to healthy, vibrant, responsible citizens. At the same time, she holds each person fully responsible for everything that happens in his or her life. Thus, everyone involved in the Delancey Street Foundation takes total responsibility for his or her choices. Importantly, this isn't done in isolation but in community. A primary ingredient to community—to *this* community in particular—is a whole lot of tough love. This includes a powerful belief in a person's capacity to grow and a commitment to joyful interdependence: *We are all in this together and so we must help each other out, just like a healthy family does.* In fact, Mimi lives in the Delancey Street apartment complex just like all of the residents. No special treatment for her or anyone else—including her children, who've been raised there and have had all of their needs met by the community that Mimi created. She views Delancey Street as a big extended family, and she is fully a part of it.

Many have thought that Mimi is standing in harm's way by living amidst the violent criminals and unpredictable outcasts who have entered the facility's doors. She sees it differently. She sees it as welcoming them into her communal family and home. She extends them her trust and in so doing earns *their* trust; as a result she always feels safe—only once or twice in nearly 30 years did she feel physically at risk.

Mimi's sense of purpose is clear: She wants nothing less than to break the frames that limit one's opportunities. Her foundation doesn't take money from the government nor does it solicit financial contributions—only donations of clothing and supplies that they can use—and she doesn't draw a salary. All of the businesses they have started, and all of the living quarters they have built—including an award-winning architectural masterpiece on some of the most expensive land in the world—were put together by Mimi and her residents with little expertise or resources. As Mimi puts it, "We've done things we didn't know we could do because we didn't know we couldn't do them."

Becoming a Resident

This intention to "figure it out ourselves" turns the whole system of welfare on its head, for the foundation's core belief is that for change to occur, it must occur from within, aided by a social environment that supports self-reliability and self-responsibility. All residents of the foundation must ask to come, although most come from parole or as an alternative to prison—often to a life sentence. Yet despite any violence in their pasts, the neighborhoods in the cities they now dwell as part of

Delancey Street have consistently been safe. In order to be accepted, they go through an extensive interviewing process and must successfully meet three conditions:

1. They must want to break their habits of cheating, stealing, violence, and drugs.
2. They must become a full-time resident, living, studying academic and vocational skills and working at a job and with each other until they are ready to leave.
3. They must live by Mimi's rules (see below).

Each resident lives in an apartment, often shared by others, on the waterfront in San Francisco or in any of the residences in other major cities (there are facilities in five other locations around the country). Each is required to get a high school degree and as part of that, take liberal arts classes. Each must train in and work at one of its businesses, including (among others) an award-winning restaurant, an award-winning moving company, a transportation and limo service, or a room for screening films and documentaries. The money earned by these businesses is pooled together and pays for the costs of living (housing, food, clothing—everything). In effect, every penny earned through its companies goes to support the education and rehabilitation of its residents. Because of this, Delancey Street has the highest rating among charitable organizations. Those who become residents must also abide by Mimi's rules, which are simple but inviolable. Anyone who breaks them either gets thrown out or goes in front of a review board (made up of residents) that decides their fate. These are her inviolable rules:

- No drinking or drugs
- No physical violence
- No threat of physical violence

In addition, the follow rules exist to guide their lives together, which, if violated, are subject to the consequence of having to do extra work such as washing dishes:

- Each one teach one
- Care for each other—be both a giver and a receiver
- Take responsibility for your actions; recognize that everything you do impacts others. Own up to your mistakes and simply fix them
- Act "as if" you can become a decent, talented person of integrity (with the expectation that doing so, you will eventually become one).

Surprisingly, few people break the rules. With no drugs, alcohol, lying, stealing, or cheating, food seems the only excess. The peer support system is so powerful that residents "get it" instantly, and work hard to be worthy of staying in the organization.

It's the Whole System that Makes the Difference

Mimi has created a self-sealing, frame-breaking social system designed to shift the mindset and conduct of troubled souls. It's a brilliant work of art, and its many components defy conventional wisdom. It is clearly not welfare, for there are no handouts. It's much more than workfare as well, even though work is part of it and people must help themselves in order to stay. Her system focuses on creating a powerful social container, much like a family, where people can become healthy and whole. By living together under house rules designed for social and emotional health, by working together in a way that teaches collaboration, service, and specific skills that translate well to the outside world, and by honoring each person's innate ability to live well with one another if given the right conditions, thousands of people have graduated Delancey Street no longer the troubled souls they once were.

In short, Mimi and her system teach the basics of life. In her words, "To be classy on the outside, you have to be classy on the inside. We teach the importance of helping one another to take responsibility. We teach that you can't change others, but you can change yourself." Over 15,000 current and former residents can lay claim to the system's power and potency—a true model of self-governance with a wide range of spectacular successes. And while she didn't say it directly, she implied in all that she shared with me that self-compassion and self-esteem were at the root of her work to support others in raising themselves from their past. By every definition, Mimi has taken the art of leadership to a new level, and she couldn't have done it without a rock-solid sense of self and a belief that anything is possible.

A Home Inside

There is a place inside each of our psyches that is home. As a child we knew it well. It's a place where we are free, alive, joyful, and fulfilled. It's a place where we connect easily with others and where we are extraordinarily creative and productive.

Over the years, through a series of conscious and unconscious choices in which other parts of us took over—our inner controller, our inner protector, our inner critic, and so on—we moved away from that place to become both individuated and conditioned. In this process of domestication, enabled by our adoption of society's rules (both written and unwritten), we progressively lost our sense of home. In asserting a position of prominence, our ego took us further away from our deeper, more natural state of being. In some ways, through this acculturation, we became more productive, but we also lost our ability to access those primary energies that were once so familiar to us. We forgot who we were, and started looking for acceptance from others.

A principal element that differentiates great leaders from others is that they instinctively know the importance of these energies. They have relaxed into the familiarity of their own inner home, they are good to themselves and with who they are, and they lead in a way that helps others find the same self-acceptance and satisfaction—to find their own golden flame. In so doing, they create conditions in their organization or sphere of influence where others can be at their best, where they are given a chance to express powerful internal energies that are both productive and deeply fulfilling. This capacity to act from the core and inspire others to do the same is more than a skill, a theory, or a model. Grounded in a deep sense of self, it's a way of being that defines great leaders.

✧

Having now become familiar with the three forces that give rise to great leadership—an inner compass, anchored in values, and a rock solid sense of self—we turn to an exploration of what leadership is all about, or, perhaps more to the point, what it could be.

KEY POINTS IN CHAPTER 8

- When you know yourself deeply and are good with yourself, you can easily be good with your weaknesses.

- Abraham Maslow's view of the self-actualized person is closely akin to being rock solid in oneself.

- The more I accept myself fully, the more I am comfortable with others not agreeing with me.

- Being judgmental toward self and others takes one further away from remarkable leadership.

- All healing comes from self-compassion.

CHAPTER 9

---- ◇ ----

LEADERSHIP AND THE SOUL

The task of leadership is not to put greatness
in humanity but to elicit it, for the greatness
is already there.

—John Buchan

So much of what I have learned about leadership leaves me wanting more. For example, in reading about it I find myself no wiser. Is it because of how I am reading the material, or perhaps, as researchers and writers try to reduce it down to essential elements, the poetry of leadership has become lost?

Fortunately, that poetry was evident in the leaders I met, but it was not only their words that inspired me; it was the palpable conviction behind them. To understand what I mean, we will need to explore more deeply the nature of leadership, to find its soulful core. We will need to understand what it has meant in the past, what it means now, and what it could mean in the future.

Leadership is a word that, while steeped in the psyche of the human condition, has so many meanings and is used in so many ways that it defies shared understanding.[1] Management, by comparison, is a much clearer concept. To manage implies the exercise of control in service to a specific outcome. Interestingly, the derivation of the word "manage" gives us clues to its meaning. It comes from the Latin *menare*, which means, "hand."

Originally the word was used to refer to horse trainers who "handled" the horses, and from there it's a short leap to images of "whipping" people into shape. In a world of certainty, predictability, and gradual change, good managers are quite useful for getting things done on time and on budget. And they will always be needed, but as change and uncertainty become the dominant themes of business, the need for leadership comes to the forefront, appropriately occupying so much of our daily concerns in organizational life.

At one time leadership and management were often thought of as synonymous terms, and the job of a leader was to manage (or coax) others to do their work—to get them to a certain place, to get them to do the job. But in this day and age, leadership is so much more than management, and at the same time still ill defined. To one person, it still is the same thing as management. To another, it may imply inspiration. Some believe it has to do with setting vision and direction, while others see it as taking charge. Years ago, the legendary organizational consultant Warren Bennis offered a popular distinction in saying that managers do things the right way while leaders figure out the right things to do.[2] Bennis was sending a message that to be a great leader, one must be guided by a vision. This earned some cache at the time, yet as a definition, it's incomplete; I don't want to reduce leadership to such a simple description.

One could say that leaders are simply people who others follow. Anyone with followers becomes, automatically, a leader. Not only is such a definition tautological, it leaves a hollow space in my heart, for thinking that a leader's sole mission is to attract followers doesn't satisfy. Further complicating this definitional landscape is that we're not just interested in any kind of leadership but in what makes a *remarkable* leader. When you add the qualifier "remarkable" you are in muddy territory indeed, for, at the most basic level, great leadership is largely characterized by one's values and goals, and these can be as varied as the individual.

Take the goal of "extraordinary accomplishment," for example. This is what charismatic leadership often seeks. Yet while such leaders can inspire others to produce astonishing things, it usually extracts a high price from those on the front lines. History is riddled with leaders who attracted willing followers motivated by fear or dependency or ignorance who fared poorly in the bargain. Hitler, for example, inspired millions of Germans to a place they otherwise wouldn't have gone, and the damage was nearly terminal. And how about Jim Jones? Was he a great leader? He meets the definition of inspiring people to follow him to a land of extraordinary riches, and failed with horrific results.

Let's consider financial performance as another measure of good leadership. Many leaders have fattened a bottom line, but have their means and motives always been honorable? At the turn of the 20th century, John Rockefeller was the richest man in the world. To some, he was an extraordinary leader. To others, he was a master manipulator who used unfair tactics to control the oil industry. Rockefeller forged an unethical (albeit, at the time, legal) alliance with a major railroad whereby they were only allowed to ship his oil and no one else's. In so doing, he significantly reduced his distribution costs (the oil industry's biggest expense) and created a virtual monopoly. Later, the Sherman Anti-trust act was created largely as an antidote to his clever and unfair tactics.

Because the meaning of greatness is relative, an authoritative definition of great leadership is elusive. As long as people value different things, we are left with enormous variety about what great leadership is or isn't. And so to say that great leaders inspire others to do great things is not quite enough. What is considered "great"? What value system does a particular "great" represent? The search for a definitive answer, at least trying to logically find one, can seem fruitless. Is there a "there" there?

Lessons from the Past

Most current and recently retired leaders of Fortune 500 companies grew up with a model of leadership built on the values of power and authority. They tended to revere the tough, silent types like John Wayne who led with their fists and who never would admit to others (or themselves) their vulnerability. To be a good husband also meant bringing home the bacon while their stay-at-home wife modeled herself after Betty Crocker or Doris Day—making a clean and healthy home and supporting her husband. These women tended to revere the same leaders as their husbands, for there were very few female role models suggesting otherwise. Golda Meir, a principal architect of the new Israeli nation, was a rare exception, but even the extraordinary Eleanor Roosevelt took a back seat to her famous husband.

Commercials in this time gone by depicted happy families who kept up with the Joneses next door. Success was measured by dollars and cents, status, and who you knew. If you owned a better car, could afford that nicer house, and could keep the lawn manicured, you were living the good life, or at least the mythology that the times implied. TV shows such as *Leave it to Beaver* and *Father Knows Best* were all the rage, cookie-cutter sitcoms suggesting that homogeneity and happiness went hand in hand.

The business leaders of this generation were deluged by these images. If you asked them to describe their personal goals, most would talk in terms of "bigger is better," "money is power," and "getting to the top" as measures of success. Achievement at all costs reigned supreme.

Leaders influenced by the mythology of this era typically built organizations in the image of machines, where each part was a cog in a vast and interconnected system. They chased goals of efficiency, economies of scale, and market clout. They patterned their companies after the top-down efficiency of the military they often served, and these very same structures were crucial in bringing this country out of the Great Depression and into the power of post-WWII prosperity.

These images are, to some extent, appropriate for they were shaped at a time where the world was relatively stable, where you could reasonably predict what might happen in the near future by extrapolating from the past. The gods of business past knew that efficiency reigned supreme and organization size was an important source of economic clout. In such a world, leaders led with a mighty sword and a commanding style. A humorous story will perhaps illustrate the point.[3] Andrew Carnegie, one of the captains of industry in the 19th century whose wealth was forged in the steel industry, was showing a group of interested parties through one of his plants when he stopped to talk to a grey haired elderly employee. "Let's see, Wilson," he asked, "exactly how many years have you worked for me now?"

"Thirty-nine, sir," came the man's proud reply, "and might I add that in all those years, I only made a single rather small mistake."

"Good work," grunted the gruff steel magnate, "but from now on, do try to be more careful!"

Such were the images that defined the past and which continue to influence, consciously or unconsciously, many of those who lead the most revered organizations of today.

My father was a typical member of this past generation of leaders. His parents went through the Depression, barely eking out a living. To my grandparents, who both emigrated from Eastern Europe, the most important thing that a person could do was to provide food and shelter for their family. My father took up that sword with a passion and drove himself to succeed, vowing at an early age not just to provide food and shelter but to create an easier life for himself and his children than his parents were able to provide for him. And so with little financial support he became a self-made man. He put himself through college and graduate school and eventually became enormously successful as one of the top stockbrokers at Merrill Lynch. I am proud of my father for what he accomplished and derive much of my resourcefulness from his example.

At the same time, we see the world through a very different lens. When I graduated from college with no idea of which profession I would choose, he gave me a present, carefully wrapped in elegant paper. "Open it, son," he said with a great deal of pride, knowing he was giving me a true and meaningful gift from the bottom of his heart. I gingerly did so, and to my surprise and befuddlement, I found it was the latest book of labor statistics from the U.S. Department of Labor.

"Here are all the classified jobs and what they pay," he explained. "Most importantly, you can see which professions are on the rise and which are on the decline. Now that you've graduated, I urge you to pick a profession that is growing, for those are the ones that will pay handsomely in the future."

I was immediately stunned. I wanted a career that was fulfilling and cared little about its monetary value. To me, the meaning of the gift rang hollow, yet to him, he was being a good father, providing me with the best guidance he knew. "Go where the money is," was his message, for money is the most important measure of success.

Sadly, I was not very appreciative. I closed the book immediately and said unequivocally, "I'm not interested in this, dad. I will not, nor will I ever, make a career choice based on money. I'm going to follow my own heart and trust that whatever I do, I will do it well, and money will naturally follow. Thanks, but no thanks."

Not surprisingly, he was deeply hurt by my reaction. I had rejected his gift and the very values upon which he had diligently built a life. But my soul had no other choice, for it did not care about money, status, and material wealth. It only cared that I live a purposeful life and fulfill my destiny, and there was no way I would find my path from reading this book. I may not have known what my soul wanted at the time, but I knew that my real job was to find that out. Ironically, in reflecting on how quickly I rejected his gift, I have come to realize that I felt free to claim my own path in part as a result of his hard work, unencumbered like he was by poverty or vestiges of the Great Depression. For the freedom that he and his efforts afforded me, I am deeply grateful.

At the time, though, we were more than a generation apart. We were a paradigm apart as well. The paradigm of leadership of the past generation had to do with command and control, with power for its own sake, with status and financial wealth. Science became a fierce and powerful economic driver, creating the greatest explosion of innovation in the history of humankind. Had I lived in my father's time, I might not have questioned this paradigm. But now, facing its consequences in the form of oppressive power structures, global warming, resource depletion, war, and poverty, I question many of the assumptions that this paradigm was built on.

The Changing Nature of Leadership

The qualities and characteristics of successful leaders have changed dramatically over the last half-century as we have moved through at least two significant business climates and are now entering a new era of business and organizational life. The ability to manage and control was the first model that described great leaders. This leadership paradigm had roots in a worldview set forth by the French philosopher Rene Descartes in the 17th century, who coined the now famous phrase, "I think, therefore I am." He viewed the human world as a complex machine that could be understood by breaking it down into its component parts. He believed that there was a natural order of things, described in terms of specific causes and effects. Building on this belief, the challenge of leadership and of management was to identify and master the mechanics of the organizational machine.

In the early- to mid-1900s, when efficiency was the primary driver for business success, the Cartesian model worked beautifully. Ushered into its full effect by Frederick Taylor's theories on scientific management and Henry Ford's brilliant innovation of assembly-line production, command-and-control leadership ruled the day, aided by the relatively stable conditions of the times.

In the latter half of the 20th century, however, the world began to speed up and people started to recognize that viewing organizations as machines often degraded the human beings who worked in them. As this occurred, new models that described organizations as organic or human systems began to take hold. In this climate, participative leadership theories began to emerge that captured the attention of business leaders. The importance of having a "vision" and fostering a strong "culture" took root as well, popularized by such books as *Corporate Cultures* by Terry Deal and Allan Kennedy[4], *Change Masters* by Rosabeth Moss Kanter[5], and *Built to Last* by Jim Collins and Jerry I. Porras[6].

Now we live in a post-modern world where knowledge, information, and fluid structures have become the keys to success. In such a world, old theories of leadership get turned on their head or thrown out altogether. "Servant leadership," "collaborative leadership," and "chaordic leadership" are becoming the models that define today's successful leader. While not claiming to be the definitive statement on the subject, the hypothesis behind these new models is that while leadership styles can take many forms, the best ones will constellate around creating conditions where people can bring out their best and be fulfilled. At the same time, we really don't understand this new world of organizational life, and it's too soon to tell which of these models will rule the day.

	1900 to mid-1900s	Mid-1900s to turn-of-the-century	2000 and beyond
Organizational Form	Machine-like efficiency	Adaptable and vision-driven	Knowledge management & fluid structures
What Defines Successful Leadership	Managing and directing others toward a shared task	Providing a vision for the future – meaningfully including others in the decisions that directly affect them	**?**

Table 9-1: The Evolving Paradigm of Leadership

While models of *good* leadership are now being re-shaped, models of *great* leadership remain hard to pin down. For all my adult life I have been fascinated with the question of what constitutes great leadership, absorbing a multitude of books on the subject that never quite gave me the answer. Beyond the platitudes of vision, empowerment, compassion, and service, little is understood about what fuels extraordinary leaders. This is not to say that these books don't offer something meaningful on the topic. They do, but for me they feel sterilized; too many books depict leadership in heroic terms or in ways that suggest superhuman abilities. They cast leadership in idealized shapes. A realistic view of leadership must acknowledge the contours and rich complexity of human doubt and frailty. My experience coaching and working intimately with many CEOs reflects paths of leadership that have been fraught with struggle, uncertainty, and insecurity. Why is there such a gap between what I read in these books and what I know to be true on the ground floor of the leadership journey?

A More Soulful Form of Leadership

Although many of the leaders of generations past defined great leadership in terms of might and accomplishment, I suspect they had a different perspective when approaching the end of their life. When faced with such finality, I would imagine that many reconsidered their prior assumptions about success. At the end of life so many measure their life not by the toys they accumulated or the power they amassed but by the good they did for society and the love they shared and were offered in return. It's an ironic observation when you consider the enormous amounts of time and energy they spent seeking goals that in the end became rather meaningless.

It's also important to note that most of these same leaders were men, propagating a highly masculine view of leadership where status, bigness, and making money were often at the core of what drove them, abetted by a culture that endorsed these values. I'm not saying that remarkable leadership has no room for healthy masculine energy. Indeed, that innate masculine drive to produce results was embodied by all of the leaders I interviewed for this book, male as well as female. But their efforts were carried out in service to a higher aim, not as ends unto themselves. This higher aim has two key qualities: to positively impact society in some way, and to positively impact the people in their companies.

In the end, a purely masculine model of leadership is no less imbalanced than a purely feminine one. "Golden flame" leadership blends the beauty and characteristics of both into an integrated whole—the masculine drive for results gets reflected in a determination to break the frames of the past, while the feminine desire to nurture, relate, and cultivate fulfillment gets reflected in how these leaders treat others.

It is no surprise then, that the leaders I met on my journey spoke little about management and material things and a lot about helping others live more satisfying lives, beginning with their place of work. Their attention is not only on economic wealth but on social and spiritual wealth as well. They don't teach us strategies for winning the game of business but for winning the game of life.

> *Great leaders don't teach us strategies for winning the game of business but for winning the game of life.*

While there is no doubt that Jack Welch ("Neutron Jack" in his younger days), Alfred Sloan, and John D. Rockefeller knew something about leadership, their counsel has clear limits when scrutinized by our heart and soul. No leadership effort can endure when it breaks the human spirit in the process. Such "tough-nosed" approaches deny the reality that human beings are complex creatures with thoughts, feelings, and amazing potential. Beating the other guy to a pulp might define success in the short run, but it's not a sustainable model for it does nothing to inspire or uplift.

Almost without exception, I have been deeply moved by how the leaders I interviewed take a more holistic approach to leadership and serving humankind. They offer a far more satisfying view of what leadership can be—what I would call "soulful" leadership—than the caricatures that we've become used to. And by focusing on these deeper aims, all of these leaders have been extraordinarily successful as defined by conventional measures of performance. They produce remarkable products and achieve significant financial success.

When I speak of "soul" I'm referring to one's essential nature, the individuality imprinted at the deepest level of their being. Soul is beyond our personality. It defines the "real me"—our most natural, primitive, wild self, the self that can never be tamed or bridled by social convention. When I spoke earlier in the book about the critical importance of tapping into one's inner authority, I was alluding to this. I believe that the wellspring from which inner authority derives is one's soul—one's deeper nature, and I believe it is formed early on.

I had a glimpse of this connection between inner authority and soul from a conversation between me and my son, Josh, who was about 7 years old at the time—an exchange that magically offered a unique perspective on life for me. One day Josh asked me, "Is everything art?" My reply was so certain that it amuses me to this day the arrogance I sometimes feel in believing I know more than a young child. In this moment, I got taught that I have so much to learn and my children so much to teach. In reply, I said simply, "Not everything."

"What isn't art?" my son asked, still deeply curious.

I thought for a moment and then pointing to the bed beside him, I said, "That's not art."

With amazing assurance, Josh replied, "Yes it is. It's someone's masterpiece."

In this moment I started to feel myself challenged and piqued by my son's amazing inquisitive nature. In spite of his curiosity, I maintained my stance of confidence. "Well, you're not art."

Without missing a beat, he said to me confidently, "Yes I am. I'm God's masterpiece."

Now in our family, we don't talk about God in the way many families that are religious do. Ours is a different relationship to Spirit such that God or the bible has never been a centerpiece. So you can imagine my surprise when he made this comment in such a matter of fact fashion. Wondering where such a beautiful notion came to him, I asked, "Who told you that?"

Speaking in a tone that suggested he was puzzled that I would even ask, he replied, "I told myself that."

Such is the wisdom of a child and the wisdom of the soul. In his bestseller, *The Soul's Code*,[7] James Hillman speaks eloquently on the concept that our calling in life is deeply coded in us and that it's our mission in life to realize its message. He calls it the "acorn theory," the idea that our lives are formed by a particular imprinting, just as the oak's destiny is contained in the tiny acorn.

This is the same notion embedded in the ancient Greek concept of *arête*. Arête was one of the Homeric Age's most important contributions to Western culture. It means to strive, to excel, and to be the best one can be. In essence, arête suggests that all sentient beings have a unique imprint designed into them, and it is the job of that being to find it and live a life consistent with it.

In Homer's epic poems, "The Iliad" and "The Odyssey," arête is frequently associated with bravery but more often with mastery. Men and women are often described as being committed to the highest levels of engagement and impact; they use all their knowledge and abilities to fulfill their greatest capability. In Homer's poems, even nonhuman beings such as noble horses and powerful gods can possess arête. In early Greek education, arête became synonymous with self-fulfillment or self-realization in terms of human excellence. Living with a spirit of arête is to seek our soul's deepest nature or desire.

Finding and living from one's soul is no easy task, though. Indeed, most people spend a lifetime disconnected from their soul. In an interview, Bill Plotkin, a wonderful depth psychologist and leader of nature-based personal growth programs, said this about the soul:

> *Each thing — "each stone, blossom, child," as the great poet Rainer Maria Rilke writes — has a soul. But only we humans, as far as we know, develop a form of consciousness that is separate from our souls. This is a distinguishing feature of humanity, at once our greatest curse and our greatest blessing: After about age four, our egos (our consciousness) are centered in a part of our selves separate from our souls so that we don't consciously understand our own unique individual essence. An initiation process is required for our egos to make contact with our souls. All nature-based cultures, from the beginning of the human story, have provided their people with such initiation rites so that each person can discover their particular way of belonging and the*

*unique gift they might offer to their human community
and to the larger more-than-human world.[8]*

Sadly, in Western society, there are no such initiations, and we end up following lesser desires that are disconnected from our truest longing. We make career choices to meet financial needs (or what we *believe* are needs). We seek to fulfill the dreams of our parents whose expectations (that we become a doctor, lawyer, member of the clergy, or some other prestigious or "respectable" role) pressure us from childhood. Our culture defines what is suitable or acceptable. When we follow some definition of success other than our own, we are not lit up. Our flame grows ever dimmer. I would argue that many examples of psychological disease are a direct result of not following one's inner compass of purpose.

Leaders who have discovered their unique gifts exhibit passion and purpose in their work and in their leadership. They create organizations where those who work there become intoxicated by that exuberance. These leaders can be charismatic or exhibit a powerfully quiet determination, but they all inspire others to reach beyond their ordinary selves. And they believe in the enormous potential that lives in each and every one of us. They believe we all have a golden flame inside. George Zimmer, founder and CEO of The Men's Warehouse and a wonderful model of this kind of leadership, was quoted as saying,

What creates longevity in a company is whether you look at the assets...as the untapped human potential that is dormant within [your] employees...If you ask me how I measure the results of my training program, I can't. I have to do it on...trust in the value of the human potential.[9]

To live by one's soul requires a degree of vulnerability rarely exhibited by most of the leaders who run our Fortune 500 companies. Most of them are trapped by their own expectations and by the expectations of others. Many believe that to be a good leader requires an imperviousness to pain, a certainty beyond all doubt, and decisiveness at any cost. If they feel a chink in that armor, they worry that they aren't living up to that model of perfect leadership. Others in the company reinforce this model by expecting such perfection and feeling disappointed whenever their leaders fall short—mistakes are not tolerated. Yet the willingness to be vulnerable, to lay it all on the line, to be, well, human, is what makes remarkable leaders extraordinary. When we see a leader's humanity, we are often deeply moved, and willingly join in to seek solutions when the going gets tough and there are no easy answers. Leaders who invite this kind of engagement are taking a road less traveled, but it's a road that has the potential to lead to greatness.

Joseph Jaworski, one of the leaders I met on my journey, touched me deeply in our meeting, one for which I am forever grateful, not only by what he shared with me, but how he shared it. Early on in our meeting, he described a magical moment – one that forever changed his life.

When he was a freshman at Baylor University in 1953, the largest tornado in Texas history (up to that time) wreaked havoc in the downtown area, about two blocks from where he lived. It killed 500 people in 30 seconds and injured thousands more. "It sounded literally like a thousand freight trains running through my dormitory," he recounted, bringing forth the memory in his mind and in his heart.

> I was alone in my dorm room and went out after all the noise stopped. Trees and electrical lines were down everywhere. The post office, a multi-floored building, was severed in half and the nearby AA baseball park had literally disappeared. An entire city block of buildings had collapsed into their basements because the vacuum had blown the bricks out. Cars and people were piled under the huge amount of bricks and debris. It was horrible, like an atomic bomb had hit.

Joseph's voice was quivering as the rush of feeling from his memory of the catastrophe filled him. He paused. It seemed that he didn't want to tell me the story in a disembodied way; he wanted to be fully present and for me to join him in sensing the immediacy of the moment. And then he continued.

> I was in the ROTC and one of the dozens of people selected to help rescue the people who were under all these bricks. This was a defining experience in my life. The others and I pulled the dead people out, putting them in a makeshift morgue, and rescuing those who were barely alive.

> On the one hand, I felt enormous terror and fear and horror. And on the other it was the most beautiful experience I've ever had. What I experienced was this amazing field that had formed around the people I was working with, as if we were able to work with a single intelligence. This was something I had never experienced before.

He paused again, wanting to be sure I got the whole of what he was saying.

> Time slowed down for me, and for three days and nights I didn't sleep, as everything seemed to move in extraordinarily slow motion. During this time there were countless but also seamless leadership changes. Everybody seemed to know exactly what to do without verbal communication, and if you did need to say something the other person was able to finish the sentence for you. We were just in a total flow state. I would say things or do things and the deeper part of me would be standing apart from me, looking down, saying, My God, how did you do that? Did I? I would look over my shoulder. Did I say that? Where did that come from? Something was operating through me.

Transfixed and deeply touched by his story and the emotional presence in which he told it, I wanted to understand more deeply this sense of being an instrument. "An instrument of what?" I asked, wishing I had been touched in my life so profoundly.

> Well, I call it a force, but since I was raised in the church, I guess I would say God. In essence, I see it as the force of all creativity. From that moment on, I swore up and down I would try and find out the source of that gift that I and the other people had. That was my purpose in life.

I pressed on, tears welling in my eyes at the enormity of what Joseph was offering. "I am stunned by the magnitude of that awareness," I said, and continued to listen with an open heart.

> I feel that there's an element of destiny here for me. I feel deeply about the importance of having a purpose in life. When I discovered that purpose and clicked into it, it felt like a trap had been laid, but it's also like rocket fuel, giving me a direction that guides me to this day. My life's work is all about helping others find their direction.

I wish you, the reader, could have been there at that moment, for it has forever touched my life. That field that Joseph spoke about washed over us both. In that moment, I had the sense that there was nothing separating us. He and I felt a special connection, as if we were one. Perhaps it was the way he spoke. Perhaps I was open to the moment. Perhaps it is always there, a rare interlude in the constant press of activities we call life, when two people allow themselves to experience what is ever present. All I can say is that I felt it, and I cried, quiet and deep sobs. "I'm crying because I can feel the field," I told him.

"Yes," he replied in a knowing way. "I feel it, too, with you." And then silence fell upon us for what seemed like an eternity before we could continue.

The Alchemical Nature of Remarkable Leadership

When leaders who follow their soul's desire encourage others to do the same, their golden flame burns with a more powerful meaning. In the Hindu Vedic tradition, every person is viewed as "golden"—not gold ore in the material sense but imbued with golden qualities. That is our true essence, to glow brightly even though our bodily shape may change. Old stories about the gold that is found within abound. Michael Meade spoke about this eloquently when he wrote, "In some stories, the fish asking for help appears as golden. Either a golden fish rising from the depths of the sea before some poor fisherman or a fish with a gold ring inside. There's a message in this discovery of gold from the depths. These stories are not just about the outside world. Something swims within the soul waiting to be heard and become known. Something deep and valuable remains hidden within each person; it desires to be recognized and held in awareness and cared for. Though small and subtle to begin with, the golden self can grow to surprising proportions."[10]

Similarly to golden fish, one could say that the gold-seeking gnomes and dwarfs of European fairytales were not trying to find material riches but seeking to discover their essential nature. The outward metaphor of "digging for gold" reflects the inward desire to live a life consistent with the resonance of one's soul. The alchemist's desire to turn lead into gold is a similar metaphor for the pursuit of our golden nature, to transform and become that which we naturally are. Great leaders are, in a way, like the alchemists of old, helping to transform the lead of sameness into the gold of something special. They do this when they manifest their vision, and they do this when they inspire others to manifest their own.

> *Great leaders are like the alchemists of old, helping to transform the lead of sameness into the gold of something special.*

Because many charismatic leaders often appear the same as what I consider to be remarkable leaders, it's important to distinguish between the two. Charismatic leaders rely on the magnetic quality of their personalities, and, to be sure, many of the leaders I met in my journey were charismatic. Their presence was palpable, and their strength of resolve attractive. Both charismatic leaders and remarkable leaders also share the same powerful inner compass that attracts others like bees to honey. The key difference, however, is that charismatic leaders, driven primarily by their egos, cultivate dependency. They want people to organize around them and follow their lead. By contrast, remarkable leaders believe that their job is to encourage others to follow their own inner compass and discover their own purpose and leadership potential. They do not fall into the dependency trap.

Remarkable leaders know that in *demanding* loyalty, others would have to subordinate themselves to something that may not be true for them. And so there was no talk among those I interviewed of tricks they used to get results or to inspire others to be better—even though that is exactly what happens when these leaders bring their essence and their power forward. Instead, they talked about the things they believe are worth caring about, and how important it is for the people they work with to have the freedom to be who they are. In so doing, they inadvertently unleash the potential in their employees, and the results speak for themselves.

Put another way, it's not just the actions of great leaders that make them great; it's also the destination they offer that is special. I'm not talking about a location in time and space. I'm talking about a goal that cuts across all boundaries, geographies, civilizations, races, cultures, and ages—to live a satisfying and meaningful life. And so in the end I want a definition of leadership that embraces this quest for soulfulness and that acknowledges the poetic journey into the heart of what we all yearn for.

> *I'm talking about a goal that cuts across all boundaries, geographies, civilizations, races, cultures, and ages – to live a satisfying and meaningful life.*

Soulful Leadership in Action

Life wants to unfold, to learn, to become. Notice when we are most alive. It's often when we experience an expansiveness of some kind—holding a baby, staring at the ocean, reaching a milestone in our professional lives. This sense of immediacy and bigness reflects an expression of our soul's desire. I also believe that, at its most basic level, our attraction for great leadership reflects a longing for guidance to fulfill that same desire. Joel Barker, a writer who speaks eloquently on the subject of paradigms and leadership, got it close when he said a leader is someone who takes us to a place where we could not go ourselves. [11] Peter Drucker said, "Leadership is not magnetic personality—that can just as well be a glib tongue. It is not 'making friends and influencing people'—that is flattery. Leadership is lifting a person's vision to high sights, the raising of a person's performance to a higher standard, the building of a personality beyond its normal limitations." [12] I believe that Drucker's words affirm the definition of remarkable leadership—creating a context where others can fulfill their soul's desire.

> *A leader is someone who takes us to a place where we could not go ourselves.*

One might legitimately ask: Why should the soul matter if the values of the past have brought us so much in the way of technological progress, financial success, and material comforts? The answer: It's the missing ingredient in the formula for leadership greatness. Without using the words directly, almost all the remarkable leaders I met had committed their lives to helping others—those they employed and those they served—to experience personal and professional fulfillment.

> *Why should the soul matter if the values of the past have brought us so much in the way of technological progress, financial success, and material comforts?*

Take Chauncey Starr, for example. The powerful purpose of the company he created, the Electrical Power Research Institute (EPRI), was to "keep the lights on." For everyone at EPRI, this has specific meaning—to do everything in his or her power to make electricity a reliable, safe, and cost effective tool throughout the world. Judith Rogala measures her success not by the size of the organization she created but by the positive impact she has on her staff through trust, inspiration, and care. Mimi Silbert has devoted her life to helping others in need find the golden flame that lives within them.

Each of these leaders challenges the prevailing assumption that says great leadership has something to do with size, money, and prestige. And because few of them seek the celebrity of leadership, they are not on the radar screen of headline news.

In its essence, to fulfill one's deepest desire is the true American dream. It's not about having a big house or a fancy car but about living life on our own terms. Chris Chavez, echoing many of the leaders I met, described it this way:

> *If a person gets out there and works hard, works smart,*
> *and is willing to play by the rules and do everything that*
> *needs to be done, he or she can enjoy success. Grounded*

in the idea of the American dream is the belief that nothing is impossible, that good things can happen to those who work hard, take care of themselves, and take their own path.

And so we can now begin to answer the question of what defines great leadership. First, great leaders create cultures where people *choose* to produce great results. And second, they create conditions where people are free to follow their own muse, just as these very same leaders followed theirs.

	1900 to mid-1900s	Mid-1900s to turn-of-the-century	2000 and beyond
Organizational Form	Machine-like efficiency	Adaptable and vision-driven	Knowledge management & fluid structures
What Defines Successful Leadership	Managing and directing others toward a shared task	Providing a vision for the future – meaningfully including others in the decisions that directly affect them	Creating a culture that encourages great results and creating conditions where others can follow their own soul's desire

Table 9-2: The Future of Leadership

The central notion here, not to be lost, is that the leader's job is to create a crucible within which the alchemical process of transformation can occur. This is a metaphorical container that both borders the organization while encouraging others within those boundaries to express themselves fully and freely. The boundaries of the container are the organization's vision, values, and fundamental strategic philosophy. The conditions for freedom are created through the principles and actions of the leader, each of which foster honesty, learning, growth, striving toward excellence, and shared effort. Within the container, everyone expresses his or her individuality while working together toward a common cause.

I am a part of a growing number of men and women who enjoy and take part in drumming circles. In them, someone will begin a beat, a unique beat that is his or her own, and then another joins in, not quite copying that beat but sensing its rhythm and finding their own complementary and unique expression of it. A third, a fourth, and then the rest join in until all are drumming or shaking their rattles or clacking their claves (thick hardwood dowels). The key to the experience is that everyone finds his or her unique expression while simultaneously listening to and feeling the beat of the entire group. It requires the capacity to honor one's own voice while being exquisitely attuned to the voices of others. When it works, it's an extraordinary improvised symphony. Similarly, resolving and harnessing the creative energetic tension between the individual and the community is a hallmark of great leadership. It requires the ability to create group alignment through vision and direction while simultaneously unleashing people's individual talents and gifts.

> *Resolving and harnessing the creative energetic tension between the individual and the community is a hallmark of great leadership.*

I believe that Costco's Jim Senegal is a great example of such leadership. He embraces a model of balance between people and results that are helping to define this new era of leadership and organizational life. For example, in contrast to WalMart's parsimonious approach to employee compensation, Senegal believes that by paying well and offering generous benefits, employees are more likely to give their best. While investors sometimes raise concerns that such generosity eats into profit margins, Senegal has remained steadfast. He is committed to creating a workplace where all can thrive, and where shareholder value is seen as a long-term proposition. Such an attitude pays huge dividends: Customers are almost always treated well, turnover is low, and shareholder return has outperformed the overall stock market. Senegal also is paid less than 90% of his peers, even though Costco ranks among the top 30 in revenue among American companies. Commenting on his comparatively low wage, he says, "I just think that if you're going to try to run an organization that's very cost-conscious, then you can't have those disparities (of paying the CEO astronomical wages). Having an individual who is making 100 to 200 or 300 times more than the average person working on the floor is wrong."[13]

Leaders who trumpet their own prowess and who argue for outrageous salaries often have difficulty generating loyalty and commitment on the part of their employees. For good reason, the disparity between wages at the top and wages at the bottom creates a continental divide between staff and executive management. Leaders like Senegal have few such problems because they place the highest importance on the culture they are creating and the long-term viability of the organization as a whole—shareholders, employees, and customers combined.

Why Great Leadership So Often Eludes Us

I believe that there are three fundamental reasons why people don't understand the essence of great leadership. First, most people seek great leadership by looking only at a leader's outer accomplishments, but such accomplishments can occur without that leader's involvement. Leadership can help get the job done, but so can competent management, a good set of instructions, and sheer will power.

The second reason why so many people miss the essence of leadership is that they look for it in a position: "Well, if they're the CEO, they must be a good leader." Many people hold positions of leadership and aren't good leaders. Remarkable leadership is about inspiration that takes us beyond ourselves. In this sense anyone can be a great leader—teachers, coaches, managers, and so on.

The third reason why great leadership is so misunderstood is that it's so hard to find. Most leaders end up in their positions not because they have great potential or great vision but because either they did in fact accomplish something that qualified them to move up in a company or because sheer longevity put them there. The problem here is that, according to the wisdom of The Peter Principle, one often rises to the level of their incompetence. Those who succeed in the current paradigm occupy many of these positions but are not able to evince the kind of leadership that shows true mastery. True mastery in leadership has to do with creating conditions where others are inspired to break the boundaries of the past and find the source of greatness inside themselves.

> *True mastery in leadership has to do with creating conditions where others are inspired to break the boundaries of the past and find the source of greatness inside themselves.*

While good leadership produces results, remarkable leadership does much more: It provides a compass for the future and opportunity for our soul to participate in that future, and that kind of leadership is rare indeed. I share Buchan's view expressed at the beginning quote of this chapter that leadership is not about empowering others, as if we pour power into them, but about drawing their own power out. To empower others implies that power doesn't already exist inside them, and in this sense great leaders never empower. Instead, they create the conditions where others' natural capacities can be fully expressed.

Almost to a person, the remarkable leaders I have met told me that truly great leadership has to do with helping others become more fulfilled, not in a material sense but from a soul sense. It has to do with going beyond the limitations of the past yet doing so in a way that also points to the future. From this definition, John D. Rockefeller, Morgan Pierpont, and the other merchant giants of late 19th century fall out right away. From this definition, any leader of any organization who focuses exclusively on wealth, power, and control doesn't qualify either.

In reflecting on what I have learned by meeting with these leaders, I have come to realize that the three forces driving great leadership—an inner compass, a powerful anchor, and a rock solid sense of self—are not isolated elements but part of a whole set. If one is missing, it becomes that leader's Achilles heel. George W. Bush is a good example. He showed ample sense of purpose—whether or not you agreed with that purpose—but fell well short as a great leader based on too many instances of questionable ethics and the impenetrable political secrecy that characterized his administration. And if you wanted to be in his inner circle, you could not question the administration's decisions, suggesting that Bush was either deeply insecure or tragically arrogant—or both. People who are transparent and secure invite openness and dialogue, not fear and submission. Similarly, Bill Clinton had the potential to go down in history as one of our greatest Presidents, but his ethical choices in the Monica Lewinsky fiasco were his undoing. No one is infallible, of course, but all three conditions must be consistently met in any definition of a great leader.

✧

How one becomes a great leader, able to embody all three forces, is the focus of our final chapters. It begins with asking the age-old question, Are leaders born or made? Some important research sheds a surprising and crucial perspective on the subject.

KEY POINTS IN CHAPTER 9

- In the past, our measures for leadership success were primarily financial.

- In the future, leadership success will have to do with shifting paradigms and with encouraging the leadership of others to break out.

- Great leaders seek to follow their own soul's code and welcome others doing the same.

- While charismatic leaders often look like remarkable leaders, they are not the same.

- Great leaders invite others to step up into their own greatness.

CHAPTER 10

———— ✧ ————

THE EVOLUTION OF LEADERSHIP

*When you were born, you cried and the
world rejoiced. Live your life so that when
you die, the world cries and you rejoice.*
—Cherokee wisdom

When I give talks on the subject of remarkable leadership, almost inevitably the question is posed: Are leaders born or made? Before exploring this question, it would be good to ask what motivates this question in the first place. On the one hand, most of us prefer equal opportunity: If we are not "born leaders," we would still like to hold out hope that we can become great leaders through the right effort or contacts. On the other hand, if leaders are "born," then great leadership is consigned to the fates, and people in responsible positions who fall short as leaders have a welcome excuse for their failures. If leaders truly *can* be made, and if leadership is hard work and not just natural talent, then each of us has the potential to step up, take responsibility for ourselves, and make an impact. I believe, and the research supports this, that they can.

Few if any of the remarkable leaders I met would say that leaders are "born." They know, all too well, how much work they have put into themselves to become who they are. They know all too well that failure—or the ability to *learn* from failures—is a necessary prerequisite for true success. They know that leadership is an ongoing process, and it requires continual openness to others and to the unique challenges of the present situation.

Some of those I met never really wanted to be in their present role. When given the opportunity to become chairman of his department in a major medical university, Larry Marton was initially disinclined. Only after considerable persuasion on the part of the dean, and after he became convinced it was for the good of the university, he accepted—and he did an extraordinary job. Later, he was offered the position of dean of the medical school at the University of Wisconsin, and again he was quite hesitant, believing that others were better suited for the job. He accepted only after the chancellor of the school convinced him otherwise. Larry shined as a leader partly *because* of his reluctance. It's not that he didn't want to lead, but he knew what was needed, honored those needs rather than personal ambition, and took the responsibility very seriously. Recall Aragorn, the reluctant king of *Lord of the Rings*. Aware of his royal lineage and heir to the throne of Gondor, he nevertheless resists his destiny—at least initially—until he feels ready to lead the kingdom against Sauron and his mighty armies.

Other leaders I met were successful precisely because they *did* seek a position of leadership, but only to accomplish a much bigger aim. They were not so much fueled by ambition, but their focus was on how to best add value through the unique gifts they had. Neither these gifts, though, nor this attitude of service, came to them overnight; they came over time, the result of their own self-reflection, maturation, and cumulative experience, combined with an ever-evolving value system.

If leaders are not born but made, is it then correct to attribute one's leadership abilities to experience? Clearly, experience—on the job and in life—can contribute to what it takes to become a great leader, but it should be equally clear that there is more to the equation. In fact, I am absolutely convinced that it is not external experiences themselves that make up who we are—it is how we reflect on and what we do with those experiences that make the difference. For example, many of the leaders I met talked about a key moment in their life when they reached a fork in the road and had to make a choice. And, more often than not, they chose the path of their humanity—their sense of honor, of care, of helping others. Their passion to make the world a better place was ignited by the needs they perceived, and these needs in turn refueled their passion.

What in their background motivated these leaders to choose such a path? There are no definitive answers, but the observation most often offered was that someone in their lives—a parent, a relative, a mentor or public figure—was a model and an example for them. To the extent that one person is a model for others, those "others" then in turn become models—in fact they may be models for *many* other people—and a powerful circle of life is created. When people in Delancey Street say, "I want to be just like Mimi," it shows the power of her leadership to be a beacon of light for others, just as her family was a beacon for her.

> *It is not external experiences themselves that make up who we are – it is how we reflect on and what we do with those experiences that make the difference.*

How Leaders Develop[1]

To help answer the question of whether leaders are born or made, we now look to psychology and, in particular, developmental theory for an understanding of how adults evolve or at least have the potential to grow and mature.

To begin, human beings act toward things and experiences on the basis of their perceived meanings. The act of writing, for example, is not just the act of putting thoughts on paper. Depending on the circumstances and reasons for writing, as well as the writer's own tastes, preferences, and abilities, writing can mean very different things to different people (or different things to the *same* people under different circumstances). To the novelist, writing may evoke the spontaneous eruption of ideas and feelings as he or she enters into a self-created world, and then communicates that world and its characters and plot lines through creative narrative styles. To the newspaper journalist, by comparison, clear and accurate gathering and communication of events is more important than creativity and imagination. And to the reluctant biology student, writing a term paper or essay might be an act of drudgery in which one feeds back information that the instructor requires.

For as long as social scientists have studied human beings, they have known that what is uniquely human is the fact that we actively participate in interpreting our world, and what emerges is our experience. This "experience" is not a static, objective phenomenon. Rather, it is a set of occurrences as seen and interpreted through our beliefs, assumptions, predispositions, and judgments. Let's refer to the totality of these psychological processes simply as our "worldview." Our worldview, in effect, is the filter through which we see and experience the world and how we define meaning. As a result, it drives our choices, which in turn produce certain outcomes, good as well as bad.

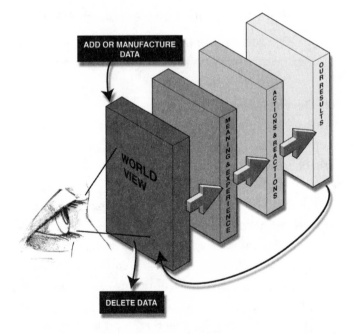

Figure 10-1: Our Worldview Filters Everything

Unfortunately, as Einstein wisely stated, the problems we've generated cannot be solved at the same level of thinking that was used to create them. In other words, our current collective worldview created the problems, and to respond with effective solutions requires a different worldview.

While the notion that we are meaning-making machines is ancient, what is relatively new to social science is the notion that our worldview can actually mature over time in a distinct progression of stages that correspond to other aspects of human development. Although many people get stuck at certain stages and never progress further, the order in which the stages unfold is predictable, a finding backed up by a large and growing body of empirical research. With each step in human growth, a new and relatively structured stage of development or worldview emerges. Each new worldview operates as a new way of constructing and understanding the world—it represents a new inner experience of the world, and results in a new way of expressing one's feelings and ideas.

> *What is relatively new to social science is the notion that our worldview can actually mature over time in a distinct progression of stages.*

There are many theories of how adult worldviews develop over time and they are now commonly understood and accepted in the field of psychology. Perhaps the leading one is offered by "psychometrician," Jane Loevinger.[2] By studying the lives of adults and how they see, understand, and makes sense in the world, Loevinger empirically found seven major stages of adult development organized in an ordered sequence. Moving from one stage of development to the next represents, by definition, a more complete understanding of the world than the prior stages. Related research has shown, for example, that individuals at higher stages of development often have greater cognitive abilities and conceptual complexity,[3] and they tend to view the world in less dogmatic and stereo-typical ways.[4] Also, as people move up the stages developmentally, they become increasingly able to (1) accept responsibility for the consequences of their actions, (2) empathize with others who hold conflicting views, and (3) tolerate higher levels of stress and ambiguity.[5] Finally, people at higher stages are more attuned to their own inner feelings and the outer environment, and they perceive social reality more accurately than people at lower stages.

From a leadership standpoint, the fact that people at these later stages of development have a greater breadth and depth of skills to draw on is especially profound, and more recent research linking adult development with leadership effectiveness convincingly proves this. Specifically, management professor Bill Torbert, a pioneer in looking at the world through a developmental lens, explored Loevinger's stages, and in study after study, he and his associates, including myself, found a direct empirical relationship between one's stage of ego development and one's leadership capability. Below is a summary of Torbert's work, taken from a multitude of studies (including Suzanne Cook-Greuter's dissertation) that profiles the qualities of thinking, feeling, and seeing that define each stage. There are certainly stages of development prior to this, such as those described by Jean Piaget and other child-development experts, but for purposes of this exploration, we will focus on adult stages of leadership development as interpreted by Torbert.

Stage	Focus of awareness and key meaning making
OPPORTUNIST	Immediate needs and opportunities. 'What you see is what you get.' Seeks short-term advantage for self. Very short time horizons. Blame always beyond self.
DIPLOMAT	Socially expected behavior. Seeks conformity, belonging, and loyalty. Provides social glue. Fears breaking rules and any sort of conflict.
EXPERT	Seeks expertise within a consistent framework or logic – perhaps a 'vocation.' Identifies strongly with what they know and what they are perfecting. Seeks efficiency and decisions based on 'incontrovertible' facts. Strives for continuous improvement.
ACHIEVER	Seeks effectiveness and results through application of strategies, plans, and actions. Works towards given goals – feels like an initiator, but more likely to take on given goals than self-create. Sets high standards for self and others and feels guilt if failing to meet own standards. Seeks feedback.
INDIVIDUALIST	Increasingly focuses on self and experience of the moment, not goals. Understands self to be one player in complex game and sees systems perspectives. Curious about own power and its use. Increasingly questions assumptions – possibly leading to 'life' experiments.
STRATEGIST	Enjoys complexity inherent in people's differing worldviews and capabilities. Alive to the moment but holds long time frames. Seeks to harness diversity. Guided by principles. Plays many roles.
MAGICIAN	Focus is transformation of society, organization, and self. Seeks common good. Enjoys interplay of purposes, actions, and results. Is elusive, chameleon-like, and maybe powerful. Possibly saddened by inevitability of paradox in human affairs.

Table 10-1: Stages of Leadership Development

That people at higher stages of leadership development typically exhibit more effective behaviors is no longer in doubt.[6] And yet the compelling nature of this evidence has not, it seems, translated into increases in the numbers of great leaders. The reason for this, from a developmental perspective, is simply that very few leaders develop to these higher stages (i.e., Individualist, Strategist, and Magician),[7] as shown in Table 10-2 below.

Stage	% from a sample of 4,510 professionals
OPPORTUNIST	4%
DIPLOMAT	11%
EXPERT	37%
ACHIEVER	30%
INDIVIDUALIST	11%
STRATEGIST	5%
MAGICIAN	2%

Table 10-2: Percentage of Leaders Who Populate Each Stage

Ego Development and the Current Paradigm of Business

To understand what the data in this chart means, we need to look at the historical and still-dominant paradigm in business and how that affects the nature of the leaders within it. This paradigm can be characterized by the following descriptors:

1. Bigger is better.

2. The world is highly competitive and competition is good.

3. The bottom line is defined solely as profits for investors.

4. Power is located at the top of a pyramid and flows down.

5. We seek the lowest cost of land, materials, and production processes for transforming raw inputs into financially viable products without concern for long-term environmental consequences.

The prevailing leadership paradigm that flows naturally from and reinforces this larger business paradigm has the following characteristics:

1. Hierarchical—power is located at the top and accumulated among a few

2. Directive—decisions are driven downward from above

3. Goal-driven—the means to achieve the goals are much less important than achieving them

5. Analytic—problems are solved by breaking them down into parts

6. Driven by logic—reasoning is valued over intuition and feelings

What's interesting to note about this is the following: In Torbert's research, Experts and Achievers comprise the largest group of leaders (67% of his combined sample), and it is their leadership worldview that largely defines the prevailing paradigm. Most leaders believe in this paradigm precisely because they are the products of it: *They can see the world in no other way.* Their worldview not only dictates that they act consistently within this model of leadership and organizational life but assures that they will continue to re-create it.

To make matters even more self-sealing, leaders at the Expert and Achiever stages are not typically self-reflective. When organizational problems exist, they rarely look first at themselves, for they cannot fathom that the deeper source of the problem is their own mindset or leadership behavior. What they do see are *other* people underperforming, not following directions, or not taking responsibility. When problems occur, the typical leader says, "If only they could see it the way I see it, if only they did what I believe they should, then the organization would work." By comparison, extraordinary leaders at higher stages of development naturally recognize their own contributions to a problematic state of affairs and are self-reflective—and self-compassionate—enough to "own" their role in it.

> *Most leaders believe in this paradigm*
> *precisely because they are the*
> *products of it: They can see the world*
> *in no other way.*

Consistent with this notion, the leaders profiled in this book (and many others throughout the world) are providing a glimpse into a wholly new paradigm of leadership and organizational life. They prefer to inspire rather than control, to unleash potential rather than apply force. They are exploring organic forms of structure and more fluid forms of decision-making. And they seek ways to create alignment in the context of diversity. The accompanying table (Table 10-3) compares the features of the prevailing leadership orientation with those of this new paradigm.

Prevailing Orientation of Leadership	New Orientation of Leadership
Hierarchical	Collaborative
Leadership based on positional power	Leadership based on personal power (one's character, ability, and approach)
Directive	Facilitive
Goal-driven toward immediate results	Driven to create extraordinary results and experience
Analytic—solve problems by breaking them down into parts	Holistic—solve problems by seeing the whole system
Driven solely by facts and logic	Driven by logic, facts, emotion, *and* intuition
Competitive	Purpose-driven toward longer-term aims
Internally focused	Synergistic Focused on the needs of the marketplace, community and the ecosystem

Table 10-3: Current vs. Future Paradigm of Leadership

The Perils of Today's Leadership

Before making the necessary shift in organizational and leadership models (and in the quality of the leadership itself), it is first necessary to realize that *the culture of an organization is to a large extent the reflection of the mindset or worldview of the leadership.* Leadership and culture, after all, are naturally and inextricably intertwined. In study after study, one finds this to be true. To the degree you believe that culture drives an organization's performance potential (and there is ample research to support such a belief), the mindset of its leadership *also* drives a large part of corporate performance. To borrow from Einstein's quote earlier, you can't inspire a new organizational culture from the worldview of the leadership that created it. Certainly other forces are at play in shaping an organization, but none more so than the conduct and character of its leaders.

Figure 10-2: The Consciousness of the Leader Creates the Quality of the Culture

It is just short of impossible to renew an organizational culture if the existing leadership worldview remains unchanged. Many leaders wish it weren't the case, but those very same leaders often fail to recognize that the problems they see in their organization are, in no small part, a reflection of themselves.

Current   **Future**

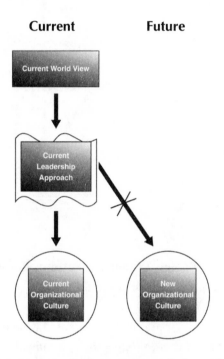

Figure 10-3: You Can't Get to a New Culture from the Old Leadership Approach

To create a meaningful shift in the conduct of an organization requires a shift in the mindset of the leadership. This is not a shift in *type* of leadership but a shift in *stage*, from one worldview to another. For the organization to mature, so must the leadership.

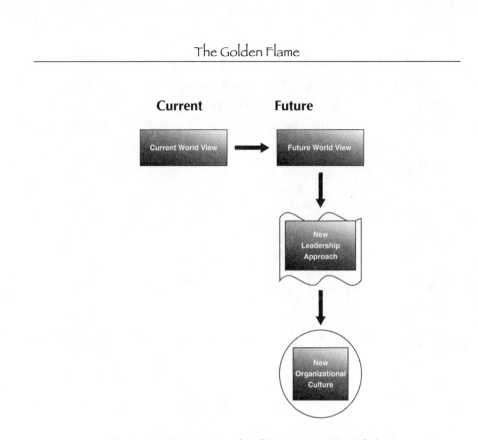

**Figure 10-4: New Leadership Patterns Result in
New Organizational Cultures**

While the prevailing paradigm of organizational leadership has achieved important advances in many areas, it may also be the source of future worldwide failure. Narrow, goal-driven efforts to achieve short-term aims, for example, turn a blind eye to the effects that such choices have on others and on the planet, leading to potential social and environmental catastrophes as well as profound injustices done to those most vulnerable. Moreover, people in positions of power rarely question the existing economic structure because most of them benefit from it. Like fish in water, they take the prevailing paradigm as a given, failing to see that the paradigm itself is the problem. Caught up in its assumptions, they cannot lead from a higher, more effective place.

Global warming, wars, and poverty are symptoms of a culture—and a species—headed for destruction. The notion that the mindset of our leadership is driving these outcomes thus has life-and-death implications. If we want to shift the culture of our planet—indeed if we want to *save* our planet—the worldviews of our leadership must shift, not just that of our business leaders but of leaders across all institutions including government, finance, education, social services, and the military, to name just a few. From a new leadership and new culture, we have the potential to create extraordinary conditions for healing ourselves while also healing the planet for present and future generations.

Finding a Solution

Unfortunately, worldviews, like paradigms, are not so easy to shift. To understand this, adult developmental theory is again quite instructive. Through an adult development lens, each stage of worldview development represents a plateau in one's life, and the forces it takes for an adult to move to a new plateau are significant.

Each stage describes a different way of being in the world—of seeing, understanding, acting, and reacting. While there are differences among stages, what is significant to theorists is the order or progression of change that underlies one's development. Loevinger, like all adult developmental theorists, is less interested in the surface manifestation of behavior than with the underlying patterns that reveal the inherent psycho-logic of each stage of development. As one acquires a new internal worldview—a new way of understanding or constructing the world—he or she reaches a new level of balance or equilibrium.[8] Once a person evolves into a new stage of development, there is a strong tendency to remain there, comfortably. Worldviews in balance understandably resist change and favor self-maintenance.

We all have a natural tendency to filter information—to selectively see and interpret the world around us. In fact, this is inevitable. Our brain cannot possibly process the billions of bits and bytes of information available to us at any given second. We naturally—and most of the time unconsciously—select what we pay attention to and prioritize for what we're most familiar with. Our worldview tends to preserve consistency—structural balance—by weeding out observations that are at odds with its way of understanding the world and attending to data that support it.

This is one of the many reasons why movements from one stage of development to another are hard to come by in adulthood. A "mature" leader, for example, who views the world in terms of absolute right and wrong, will often weed out information that implies ambiguity. Things either are true or not true, right or wrong, possible or impossible in that leader's mind. To enter into the nether zone of ambiguity feels akin to inviting internal and external chaos, and so the ego system resists any movement in that direction. As a result, most professionals, managers, and leaders plateau at the Expert or Achiever stages. In many ways, our entire Judeo-Christian tradition as well as our societal structures and systems support this very same plateau.

Waking Up to True Leadership

If the "system" seems rigged against personal growth, how does such growth occur? In spite of the stability associated with being at a fixed stage of development (especially for adults), humans can and sometimes do change, often through a series of exchanges with their environment. They not only select what is important to them from their surroundings and assimilate it into their own way of making meaning, but they also accommodate to that environment through subtle shifts in that very meaning-making system.[9] Enough shifts in one direction eventually result in a change in structure and lead to a newer, more effective way of being in and relating to the world. A rise to later stages of development, then, often requires a cultural or social environment that challenges people to think from different vantage points, to question societal and cultural presuppositions, and to break out of the mold of their social climate.

Through powerful coaching systems, leadership learning experiences, and organizational feedback—processes designed to help expand and deepen the ability of leaders to see from wider, more positive, and more confident standpoints—one's leadership consciousness can indeed shift from the prevailing Expert and Achiever levels of development to Individualist, Strategist, and Magician levels. Still, such shifts take time and don't happen overnight.

How a Shift Can Occur

Christine was the leader of a small company producing breakthrough products in the eye care industry. The company had been growing rapidly in its early days, but when I met her that growth had stagnated. While there were several reasons for the slowdown, Christine had enough self-awareness to believe that her own lack of leadership or vision may have prevented the company from going to the next level. We explored some of the causes behind her current situation and agreed that every organizational leap must start with vision. And so we spent a full day together climbing a mountain, enjoying the views, and exploring her life. Along the way, Christine discovered a vision dwelling deep inside her, aching to emerge. We met once more to coalesce her thoughts and feelings into a more clear and executable vision of the company.

The key to implementing this vision was that Christine would have to take a huge leap from a command-and-control leadership style to one that invites others to step up into their own self-authority. As all great leaders do, she discovered by insight and self-reflection that the more she held tight to the reins of her organization, the harder it would be for others to find their own inspiration and self-fulfilling path. Over the next two years, I worked with her, her senior team, and many others in the company to develop a new and higher-performing structure and process, which required Christine to shift her leadership approach. Little by little, she did, helping the organization to step up into its next phase of maturity. One of the most difficult things she did was to invite the executive team—despite their inexperience—to join her in making decisions that she ordinarily made herself. People now report that the company has really changed, transforming stagnant performance into growth and profitability and high turnover into a stable workforce. And where the company was once centered on Christine, it is now centered on the vision, the culture, and the larger team as a whole.

In spite of the relative rarity of such shifts, it happened time and again to the leaders I met. Propelled by a deep desire to make a difference in the world and by a deep belief and trust in themselves, they kept seeking challenges that required them to find better ways to communicate and to engage with their environments. In so doing, they paved the way for their development toward greatness. And while some were blessed with more intelligence than others, there is little evidence to show a strong relationship between *cognitive* intelligence (the kind most frequently measured) and leadership effectiveness. Rather, recent studies show that *emotional* intelligence (as researched and described by Daniel Goleman and others) is far more important—an aptitude earned and learned and not baked into our DNA.

> *Propelled by a deep desire to make a difference in the world ... they kept seeking challenges that required them to find better ways to communicate and to engage with their environments.*

By emotional intelligence being "earned," I mean that it's developed through a passion for self-betterment and for achieving one's purpose. Such an earning-learning process involves both intelligent self-awareness and a steep learning curve—conditions that are at odds with the "quick fix" mentality that our society demands and expects on so many levels. This addiction to easy (but ultimately ineffective) formulas is one of the reasons we have so few great leaders.

The leaders I met were also driven to understand people—not only what influences them but also what they really need. Such authentic caring didn't come easily, however; many reported a cognitive break, a "wake-up call," that entirely shifted their perspective.

I had such a call as a freshman in college while sitting in the woods, reflecting on my life. My childhood had its share of emotional pain, and the way I coped was by withdrawing into a shell. While this may have protected me, it also shielded me from deep feeling. And so under a tree, I had the sudden awareness that I did not know how to love or care for others, nor did

I feel loved by anyone. For reasons I cannot explain, I *knew* that my life would be empty if I didn't make a change. In that magical moment, I said to myself, "If nothing else, I will learn how to love," and I kept my promise. I joined an "encounter group" at age 19, went into therapy, studied psychology, and sought out people with whom I could learn. Slowly but surely I found the inner capacity to feel deeply and to love, and while this still doesn't always come naturally to me it does come much more easily.

As noted above, many of the leaders I met on my journey had a seminal moment that affected their lives. Such moments were not only life changing, they caused a shift in their internal way of making meaning, and in so doing created a powerful opening for something more. BevMo's Bannus Hudson revealed to me such a moment.

> *I've always been in a leadership position, whether in Cub Scouts or leading my college fraternity, but my style was primarily one of overpowering others. Classic kick-in-the-ass management—and just making things happen by sheer will. And if people got in my way, I'd just run over them. It's a very effective style from the standpoint of getting hired, promoted, and getting more money. But the bigger the organization I managed, the more difficult that style became. I started to experience a backlash and I couldn't overcome it. I realized I was pushing harder, working 18-hour days, and wasn't enjoying my work as much as before. Something was wrong. Fortunately for me, somebody pointed that out and I listened to him.*

I leaned toward him. "What did he tell you?"

"Well," Bannus said, "this manager said that my people didn't like me and he wanted to explain why."

I couldn't help but notice the economy with which he spoke. Sitting in front of this self-aware man, observing how the feedback struck him, I then asked, "You weren't aware that people didn't like you?"

Bannus replied with the kind of self-revealing honesty I had come to appreciate in all the leaders I had met.

"I didn't have a clue. Didn't care, actually. Why should I care? I was running the thing. I knew what needed to be done. I'm overstating it a little bit, but not a lot."

I began to wonder about feedback—why it shows up when it does, and how people tend to respond to it. Sometimes I'll disregard it and at other times I'll take it in. Curious about what was true for Bannus, I asked about this moment for him. "Why do you suppose you were receptive to his feedback at that time?"

He replied simply and candidly. "Things were getting out of control. The hours. The stress. I knew at some level that something wasn't right. That moment got me to thinking that I'd better find a different way to do things. I'm now a much better leader."

Ban Hudson is not alone; countless leaders from all over the world have had similar wake-up calls. What's distinct about this story is that Ban heeded the call. He did so because he was ready. His psychology, his deeper values, his stage of development—or perhaps the stage he was ready to raise up to—caused him to listen. These wake-up calls happen all the time. The question is, Are we ready to listen?

Our Potential to Be Great Leaders

The culture and performance of an organization is to a large extent the reflection of the consciousness or mindset of its leadership. And leadership abilities do not arise in a vacuum; rather, they arise in the course of a long process of feedback—from the environment, from others, and from leaders' own self-inquiry about their values and priorities. Such resourcefulness and responsiveness comprise true leadership, and they are almost always hard-won. This kind of leadership cannot be understood, indeed cannot *exist,* without a commitment to learning. Looked at in this way, the concept that people are "born" to lead (or not) is not only false, it's nonsensical. I agree with Warren Bennis, a wonderful researcher and observer of leadership dynamics, who said, "The most dangerous leadership myth is that leaders are born—that there is a genetic factor to leadership. This myth asserts that people simply either have certain charismatic qualities or not. In fact, the opposite is true. Leaders are made rather than born." In ways large and small, we are all leaders. And to lead effectively is a profound responsibility, requiring understanding and exploration of our deepest selves.

✧

While everyone must follow their own path, there are signposts at each step of the way. Much like the heroic journey of many myths and legends, there are patterns in a leadership journey that appear universal. It is to these patterns that we now turn our attention.

KEY POINTS IN CHAPTER 10

- Leaders are made, not born.

- It's just that they are made slowly.

- Great leaders embody the characteristics of people who have evolved and embrace a more complete worldview.

- You cannot shift a culture, a country, or the world from the same worldview that created it.

- Shifting worldviews requires many factors that are not necessarily comfortable.

- Staying in the comfort zone of one's life will unlikely cause a shift.

- We all have the potential to be great leaders.

CHAPTER 11

———— ◇ ————

BECOMING A REMARKABLE LEADER

Becoming a leader is synonymous with becoming yourself. It is precisely that simple, and it is also that difficult.

—Warren Bennis

As we near the end of the book, we come full circle in our journey toward remarkable leadership. We know the things that make great leaders great. They include vision, honesty, courage, determination, compassion, and a focus on the needs of the whole. And we know what gives rise to these forces—a person's deeper character. A powerful character is built out of three primary forces: a clear compass, a powerful anchor, and a sense of inner solidity. Knowing who you are and trusting in yourself is essential to that deeper character.

Yet we're still left with some important questions. What gives rise to such forces, and how does one discover them? Why does one person's character mature in this way, while another's does not? Why do some leaders get it in their bones, while for others it just stays in their head? Why do some choose the path less traveled and others settle for the ordinary? Many of the answers remain a mystery, but while we can't change our childhood or our past, we can start changing the choices we make right now, in this moment, and beyond. And that's how anyone can grow into remarkable leadership.

The choices we make when faced with moments of truth will either build or limit our character. Taking the road often traveled, settling for the status quo, won't do it. But following your soul's desire and encouraging others to do the same will. A deep and sustained commitment to living from one's deepest core is the straightest line to developing character.

In apologizing for their dubious behavior, many a sports hero has said, "I am not a role model. I never asked for the job." This is a statement of denial, of avoiding responsibility. They are role models, whether they like it or not. And so are we all—to our neighbors, our children, to anyone who witnesses or is affected by the choices we make. We all cast a shadow no matter how large or small. The question for our sports heroes, for the celebrities we admire, for the leaders of our institutions, and for ourselves, is not whether we are role models but what kind of role model are we.

Two Simple Guiding Principles

Among the leaders I interviewed, I observed two fundamental qualities that they all share, causing them to stand apart from the rest and making them powerful role models. The first quality is that they are inner-driven—they follow their own compass and make decisions from the wisdom they find there. This was the main point expressed in chapters three through six. It's a realm they understand, one that defines the quality of their leadership. It's also a quality that must be earned. Contrast this model to leaders who are outer-driven, who are constantly reacting to shifts in the wind, the choices of others, the latest management trend. They lack the inner conviction and clarity from which to make difficult choices. On a continuum of inner-driven versus outer-driven, great leadership would be located on the inner-driven end.

Figure 11-1: Inner-driven vs. Outer-driven

The second fundamental quality of remarkable leadership is a commitment to serving others, to being focused on *their* needs. We'll call this "other-focused." This is distinct from most leaders, whose focus is on themselves—their needs, their ego, their accomplishments. We'll refer to them as "self-focused," which is on the other end of a continuum.

Figure 11-2: Other-focused vs. Self-focused

Playing with these two dimensions, we can begin to point out some potential weaknesses of typical styles of leadership. Those who are inner-driven but self-focused, for example, are often determined to do something great but can be selfish. They accomplish much but don't inspire others. Larry Ellison, the founder and CEO of Oracle Corporation, is often accused of this, particularly among his many detractors. Leaders who are outer-driven but also self-focused try to impress others while often lacking sincerity or consistency. As a result they are often not trustworthy. I am reminded of a client who refers to a former boss as an "empty suit." The CEO in question had an enormous gift for drawing glorious images of a bright future but lacked substance as a leader. Leaders who are outer-driven and other-focused tend to be caretakers. While warm and giving, they often don't have the fortitude to make tough decisions for they are constantly trying to be liked. I am thinking of a friend who aspires to be a CEO but is getting turned down right and left for such positions. Those who know him well consider him wonderfully pleasant but also "wishy-washy." One company turned him down for CEO because they "didn't know where he stood." The only place from which great leadership derives is inner-driven and other-focused.

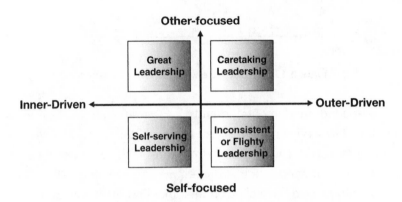

Figure 11-3: Dimensions of Leadership

> *The only place from which great leadership derives is inner-driven and other-focused.*

The Leadership Journey

Each of the leaders I met has been on a journey toward finding and then living from their core self. It is a journey across both time and space—emotional, psychological, and spiritual space—and one that leads them to their own golden flame. It is a hero's journey, which in our time requires less physical courage than the courage to face one's self. In short, it's a journey toward expanded consciousness. Joseph Campbell, a profound teacher of the meaning of myth, spoke about this journey in his book, *The Hero with a Thousand Faces.*

> *The Hero, therefore, is a man or a woman who has been able to battle past his personal and local historical limitations to the generally valid, normally human forms. Hence [heroes] are eloquent, not of the present, disintegrating society and psyche, but of the unquenched source through which society is reborn.*[1]

On the heroic journeys of the leaders I met, each faced multiple moments of truth where they had to choose between the ego's desire for wealth or prestige and a deeper desire to make a difference in the world. In facing these decisions, they went through a rite of passage that all heroes, both ancient and modern, encounter: *separation, initiation,* and *return* or *rebirth.* Separation means being cut off from the innocent certainties that have sustained you in the past but that will not help you in the future. Initiation means courageously facing a powerful challenge and accepting the potential failure in meeting it. Return or rebirth signifies the transformation of the self, in this case into a new kind of leader, guided by a steady inner flame. Says Campbell,

> *A hero ventures forth from the world of common day into a region of supernatural wonder: fabulous forces are there encountered and a decisive victory is won. The hero comes back from this mysterious adventure with the power to bestow boon on his fellow man.*[2]

My own journey began many years ago in childhood, influenced by the leadership of my mother and father, who taught me many things that have shaped who I am today. My mother, for example, taught me honesty, challenging me always to be truthful. My father taught me to believe in myself: "You can do or be anything you want, Keith." At the same time, I often experienced my parents as judgmental and felt rejected by their criticism and lack of tenderness. In many ways, I was driven to succeed by the hope of gaining their love. If only I accomplished more, I thought to myself, then they would finally be proud of me. Early on, I developed a belief that leaders should always be loving and caring, borne out of my own desire for an idealized parent.

My leadership journey continued in school, where I had high expectations of my teachers. And with few exceptions, I was sorely disappointed. My leadership disappointments extended through early adulthood as I found the managers who I reported to lacking in so many ways. As I matured, I began to realize why my search for remarkable leaders could never be satiated: I was searching for something outside myself, for someone to protect me from the storminess of life. This recognition explains a recurring nightmare I had for many years. In this dream I am a young child standing in front of a bay window in the house I lived in until the age of four, watching a raging hurricane. The wind is howling and I am shaking in utter terror. No furniture is in the house and no one is home. I know that if I cry out for help, no one will answer because no one is there.

I had this dream a couple of times a year for over thirty years, until I started my own consulting firm about eleven years ago. That decision marked the moment I finally embraced my own leadership potential and started looking for answers within. I couldn't manifest that potential, however, until I was willing to accept the judgments and even the rejection of others, which couldn't happen until I felt whole and loving inside.

As my leadership journey unfolded, I noticed that the more I healed my wounds, accepted and embraced who I am, dropped into my body, and lived from my soul's desire, the less I sought leadership from others. This process of learning and awakening and manifesting my potential certainly hasn't ended—but thankfully the nightmares have.

In reflecting on my own life and in looking at the lives of others, I have come to learn that there are three important phases in the journey toward mature and remarkable leadership.[3] Each phase must be experienced before the next one can begin (see figure 11-4).

The first phase is about openness and experimentation. The beginning of any craft, including leadership, involves experimenting with a wide range of behaviors, and often you must fly by the seat of your pants. During this phase, you figure some things out through trial and error, but it is also a period of discomfort as you realize, "This isn't as easy as I thought it would be."

> *The first phase toward great leadership is about openness and experimentation.*

The second phase of the process is often about looking for leadership wisdom from the outside. This step starts with a choice: "I don't just want to be a leader. I want to be a *great* leader." Typically, at this point, you read a whole bunch of books written by successful leaders, seeking their distilled wisdom or hoping to find a mentor. During this time, your range of behaviors narrows as you focus on imitating others and their models. Ineffective behaviors are eliminated and your competency grows. Despite the improvements, though, your leadership training feels more like a paint-by-numbers process, and you never feel quite in the groove.

Nevertheless, this is an important step, for it's where you start to develop the skill of discernment. In evaluating examples of both effective and ineffective leadership, you will idolize (and learn from) those who embody the qualities you admire and reject the ones who don't. It's a skill-building and maturation phase, for you are not yet ready to step up as a leader.

> *The second phase of the process is often about looking for leadership wisdom from the outside.*

Navigating the third and final phase requires recognition that all of the previous behaviors and efforts, the imitating and idolizing and judging and rejecting, were largely a process of *psychological projection*. The importance of this concept to leadership maturity and to maturity in life cannot be overemphasized.

We've all had the experience of coming to a snap decision about someone's character without much evidence and then relating to this person as if that conclusion was true. Later, however, we discover that our assumptions were wrong, the result, more often than not, of having projected onto this person some quality that is actually in us.

Psychologists define projection as an unconscious or unintentional transfer of our own internal psyche onto an outer object. For example, manager Susan has an employee named George who is consistently late for meetings. She is frustrated by this and, out of that frustration, reprimands him for his lax approach and emphasizes that it's becoming a big problem. What she doesn't see so easily, however, is that she is sloppy herself about meetings, often arriving late or having to reschedule at the last minute. Susan sees in George an aspect of her own personality and rejects it based on her own self-image of reliability, completely unaware of her tendencies in the same direction.

We all project our judgments, and our aspirations, on to others, often unaware that we are doing so. Consider, for example, someone you admire who seems honest and forthright. Whether or not this is so is not the question, for you can never know for certain (especially at first glance), but to the extent that you admire honesty suggests that you possess, embrace, or aspire to that same quality.

Projection is an unconscious psychological mechanism. The more that we are unaware of or refuse to acknowledge certain of our own characteristics or tendencies, the more likely we'll project them onto others, convincing ourselves that it is they, not we, who have "a problem."

In Jungian terms (as discussed in Chapter 8), that which is disowned (whether a positive or a negative quality) is our *shadow*—the part of us that we cannot yet see. By learning to identify when projection is occurring, when qualities of yourself may be peeking out from behind your own shadow, and by owning or embracing these qualities, you begin to sow the seeds of your own metamorphosis into the leader you want to be.

If you idolize people who are courageous, for example, consider for a moment that they might be reflecting your own courageous tendencies or potential. Own it and thus embody it more fully! If you find yourself judging people who are rebellious, consider the possibility there is a strong independent person inside *you* aching to get out. Perhaps it won't emerge in the form of rebellion but as a creative urge for self-expression. Such is the process of inner mastery—becoming more fully aware of that which is hard to see.

This movement toward inner mastery marks the final phase of the quest to discover your own leadership essence—the set of behaviors, beliefs, and values that are distinctively yours. It is only in this final phase when you start to take control of your destiny, for here you begin to tap into a fluidity, an ease, a capacity to make flexible choices, moment by moment, and it opens the door to your potential. Reaching this level, the level embodied by all remarkable leaders, requires that you return to yourself—to find your own home and become comfortable in your own skin. It requires a passionate desire to plumb the depths—to find, express, and live from the calling of your soul. It means that you must face your inner demons—your inner critics, doubts, and fears—for nothing less will get you there. There are no short cuts, no magic pills, no sprinkles of fairy dust for achieving the inner knowing from which great leadership emanates. And, paradoxically and equally important, you can't get there if the desire comes from ego. Your ego may have caused you to want to be a leader for all the glory and power that such a role implies, but it is that very same ego that will keep you from becoming great. Remarkable leadership is not about adding a notch to the career holster but about surrendering to all that you are in service to something greater.

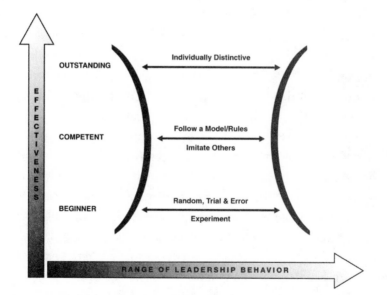

Figure 11-4: Leadership Maturation

> *The movement toward inner mastery*
> *marks the final phase of the quest to*
> *discover your own leadership essence.*

Arriving at Wholeness

At the end of this long journey one emerges into wholeness and an experience of full self-compassion. By wholeness I mean embracing and embodying all that you are and all that you are capable of. Great leaders operate from mind, body, soul, and spirit simultaneously. They may not say it in so many words, but you can sense the powerful expression of their core essence.

According to Carl Jung, the path toward wholeness has to do with *individuation*, the process of separating from others and embracing one's own uniqueness. Individuation is, to a large extent, the soul's process of waking up—of embracing itself. It is a process of journeying toward the core of who you are and wanting to live from that place. Many people justify their negative behaviors by saying, "Well, that's just me." But in saying this, they are making excuses, giving power to their neuroses or limitations. This is not individuation. Individuation requires that one go much deeper. It's the ultimate expression of living out your soul's calling.

Jungian analyst Robert Johnson, in his wonderful autobiography *Balancing Heaven and Earth*, offers an important distinction between a career and a calling. A career, he says, is something that fulfills our earthly desires for comfort or safety. A calling, on the other hand, chooses us, and the satisfactions, as well as the challenges, are of a much greater magnitude.[4] Some might say that ego drives a career while something deeper gives us a calling. There is no one formula for arriving at the destination of your soul's calling. Sometimes it finds you, much like those who are drawn by "spirit" to be ministers or priests or rabbis. Others find it accidentally, starting "a job" that eventually becomes a joy. For most people, however, finding their purpose comes at the end of a quest such as the one I've described in this book. Whatever the final step from a career to a calling, from being a good leader to a great leader, it requires that we listen to our soul and follow its urgings. Once this threshold is crossed, there is no turning back. And to cross it, you must ask yourself—and answer—some important questions:

1. What is my purpose in life?
2. What does my life stand for?
3. What is the message that my life and conduct represent?
4. How do I matter in the world?
5. What are my unmovable convictions?

| Poor Leadership | Good Leadership | The Potential for Great Leadership |

Figure 11-5: Life's Journey toward Great Leadership

Most people in leadership positions haven't answered these questions. That doesn't make them bad. In fact they are like most people. They follow the guidance of their parents, their community, their culture, and their religion, but don't know what's true for themselves separate and apart from these powerful influences. They may be "leaders," but there is much they don't know about themselves. Breaking out of these patterns isn't easy. It requires inner examination—seeing yourself with different eyes than the ones you normally see with.

> *Ego drives a career while something deeper gives us a calling.*

It also requires that we pay attention to our dreams. In the world of soul expression, dreams—those we have at night as well as the daydreams we allow ourselves while awake—can have significant meaning. Consider the following example. For a long time, Charlotte had night dreams of becoming a cartoonist. Does that mean she should do so? Well, if she has the talent for it and it gives her pleasure, then by all means. But what if she doesn't have the talent for it? Perhaps she can't draw at all. Then what does her dream mean? That her soul's calling is to make others laugh with insight and whimsy or to offer a perspective that helps people look differently at the world? These symbols and images are worth exploring, as was my recurring dream about that hurricane. They are allies in the quest for purpose and clarity.

I recently saw a movie called *Goal: The Dream Begins.* It is about a teenaged Latino from the barrios of Los Angeles who loves to play soccer and dreams of becoming a professional. His father thinks his son foolish and doesn't support the young man's dream. Then one day a former professional soccer player observes the young man playing on his local soccer field. The professional is impressed and pulls some strings to give the young man a tryout in England. When the young man excitedly presents this to his father, saying he needs to take a few days off from work, the father refuses. "This is a pipe dream," he implies, and admonishes him to "stay home and work for the family." But the boy won't let it go. He saves his money, and when he has enough to travel to England for the tryout, the boy's father steals his son's money to buy a truck so that the family can earn a better living. The young man is crushed.

A short time later his grandmother comes to him with a train ticket to the airport and a round-trip ticket to England. She had dipped into her life's savings and hocked some jewelry to buy the tickets. Her words were telling: "This is for you, my grandson. Follow your dreams."

In the movie the father represents the ego, focusing solely on protection and earthly needs and seeing no practical value in "dreams." The grandmother represents the wisdom of the soul; she knows that to live a full life, you must follow your own path—to become individuated and embrace your true nature, or at least to give it your all. She essentially says to the young man, *the truck is your father's dream, to make an honest living for the family. It has its own virtue, but it's not yours. You must go out and follow your own dream.* And that is the message of the soul.

To take this final step toward one's golden flame, introspection is crucial. Although there are many exercises for finding one's values, you have been living them all along, for better or worse. The challenge is to discover what they are. One way of doing so is to look at all of the important choices you have made in your life and ask yourself: What is the thread that holds them together? When it came down to making a decision, what values or principles guided me? After a while, a pattern will emerge offering a clue to your life purpose, shaped by the values you have unconsciously tried to live by. Another way to access your guiding motivations is to ask yourself: Who do I most admire or respect in the world and why? Looking closely at their lives will begin to reveal the principles or values that are most important to your own life, leading to a clearer sense of purpose.

As you take these final steps, it's vital to get in touch with your self-esteem, to feel good about all that you are. Some use psychotherapy to reach such acceptance, while others rely on the guidance of a spiritual advisor. Still others participate in personal growth experiences designed to challenge themselves and deepen. Regardless of the means, you'll know you have embraced yourself—that you have finally "come home"—when you are fully comfortable in your own skin, expressing your truth with ease and encouraging others to do the same.

In the end, the journey to becoming a great leader is the hero's journey. As Proust once said, "We don't receive wisdom; we must discover it for ourselves after a journey that no one can take for us or spare us." Such a journey requires a breaking away from the shackles of the past and a commitment to finding oneself—not the self of the personality but the deeper self. Few people take this journey, for it can be painful and fraught with pitfalls. Those who do, however, no matter their position or their work, are richly rewarded, for they will have truly earned their greatness.

KEY POINTS IN CHAPTER 11

- Great leaders are inner-driven and yet other-focused.

- By focusing on other leaders and their failings, we limit our own leadership capability.

- By continuing to idolize others, we miss our own true brilliance.

- You can only embrace yourself as a great leader by finding and owning your own signature as a leader.

- Our dreams can provide guidance toward embracing ourselves.

CHAPTER 12

---◇---

THE SECRET INGREDIENT

Don't ask yourself what the world needs; ask yourself what makes you come alive. And then go and do that. Because what the world needs are people who have come alive.

—Harold Whitman

What is the fundamental difference between great leaders and those who are happy to follow them? Some might say the key difference is intelligence, yet many extraordinary leaders are known for their simplicity of thought and deed. And there are many great thinkers who aren't great leaders. Others would argue that *emotional* intelligence is the key ingredient. And because many of the leaders I met demonstrated enormous emotional intelligence, one could easily agree with that. Yet there are many who display emotional intelligence yet shy away from the responsibility that great leadership requires.

Is it integrity? Perhaps, and certainly Chapter 5, which focuses on the anchor of values, makes the claim that it's a crucial ingredient. But many follow their internal compass without reaching the heights that remarkable leaders reach. How about fierce resolve? Well, again, there are many who accomplish great things but never inspire others to do the same.

In the final analysis, having met and interviewed numerous wonderful leaders, I've concluded that a key difference between great leaders and the rest of us, the secret ingredient, is that while we say "Not me," great leaders say, "Why not me?" They believe in themselves. They step up to the plate and take a big swing; and they do it in a way that inspires others to follow. Larry Flick, CEO of Prudential Insurance's Fox & Roach/Trident group, echoed the feelings of all of the leaders I met when he said, "I trusted myself."

By following their own passion and meeting every obstacle, great leaders demonstrate a belief in themselves and the ability to get beyond their self-doubt and inner critic. When those doubts are replaced by a strong sense of self, profound leadership skills naturally emerge. Such people put themselves in harm's way. They are willing to fail, and fail big. Mimi Silbert of Delancey Street said it simply: "It just made sense to me, and so I did it." One of the CEOs I have worked closely with counsels his executive team to "move toward the danger," to step into the fray and find a way to make a difference. And that is what great leaders do. They may flinch when faced with a tough challenge, but they meet it anyway.

The phrase, "If it's meant to be, it's up to me," is close to capturing the essence of the secret ingredient of which I speak. But even that is not quite enough. What's missing is the fact that remarkable leaders don't do it alone. Instead of "Follow me," they say, "Join me." They stand out for their ability to enroll others in a powerful cause—*their* powerful cause. There is a saying I once heard that captures this beautifully: *Great leaders are always willing to go it alone, and they never go it alone.* This has all to do with the message in this book. The inner compass of great leaders gives them purpose. Their rock solid sense of self allows them to put that sense of purpose out there with clarity and conviction. The combination inspires others who share that purpose to join them. Their integrity inspires trust and ultimately commitment. It is in this way, the combination of the forces creates the elixir that invites true commitment to a cause. Interestingly, the word commitment comes from the Latin word *committere*, which literally means to join, connect, and entrust. *Com* means "together" while *mittere* means "to send." Originally, the word *committere* meant to send together into battle.

The ability to inspire commitment is rare and yet well embodied by great leaders. It starts with one's own commitment and naturally flows from there. It is the thing that truly differentiates them from others and is what causes us to say, "Now there's a great leader." Scott Johnson embodied this stance when he chose to start his own company. He had little resources and no experience, just a dream to change the course of research in the medical industry and a belief that he could do it. No amount of money could match the powerful determination that burned in his heart, a determination that required he share his quest with others.

> *A key difference between great leaders and the rest of us, the secret ingredient, is that while we say "Not me," great leaders say, "Why not me?"*

In thinking of Scott Johnson, I think about how one must trust oneself fully to be a great leader. The inspiring words of Marianne Williamson come to mind:

> *...Our deepest fear is not that we are inadequate. Our deepest fear is that we are powerful beyond measure. It is our light, not our darkness, that most frightens us. We ask ourselves, who am I to be brilliant, gorgeous, talented, fabulous? Actually, who are you not to be? You are a child of God. Your playing small doesn't serve the world. There's nothing enlightened about shrinking so that other people won't feel insecure around you. We are all meant to shine, as children do. We were born to make manifest the glory of God that is within us. It's not just in some of us; it's in everyone. And as we let our own light shine, we unconsciously give other people permission to do the same. As we're liberated from our own fear, our presence automatically liberates others.* [1]

The light that Williamson refers to is really no different than the metaphor of the golden flame I have used throughout this book to characterize remarkable leaders. The inner quality they have brought into the world inspires others to step up and live from the flame that burns brightly inside of them. And this flame can burn no matter your age. Witness the young Samantha Smith, the 10-year-old girl who naively wrote a letter to Soviet General Secretary Yuri Andropov in 1983 that became one of the main catalysts for breaking down the Berlin wall. *"Dear Mr. Andropov,"* she wrote,

> *My name is Samantha Smith. I am ten years old. Congratulations on your new job. I have been worrying about Russia and the United States getting into a nuclear war. Are you going to vote to have a war or not? If you aren't, please tell me how you are going to help to not have a war. This question you do not have to answer, but I would like to know why you want to conquer the world or at least our country. God made the world for us to live together in peace and not to fight.*
>
>

Sincerely,
Samantha Smith

Andropov was touched by the letter and invited young Samantha to visit the U.S.S.R. with her parents in July 1983, when the Cold War was beginning to heat up again. They toured many places, including the city of Leningrad and a youth camp on the shores of the Black Sea. Major television networks covered the visit with nightly reports, and Ted Koppel interviewed Samantha on ABC's *Nightline.* After her travels, she innocently declared during a Soviet press conference that Russians were "just like us."

Her singular unassuming act is a powerful testimony to the potency of the principle of trusting one's natural impulses. In her own sweet way, she was basically asking, "Why can't the U.S. and U.S.S.R. get along?" Her visit and her concern inspired many others to seek opportunities for exchanges between the two countries, and eventually the Soviet people, who were seen as our enemy, appeared very human and the Cold War began to thaw. Subsequent efforts by Mikhail Gorbachev and many others finally tore down the Iron Curtain, the invisible wall that surrounded the U.S.S.R. for decades. Before that Curtain could fall, though, the human walls of divisiveness had to be torn down, and young Samantha Smith showed the way.

I can remember countless times early in my life when I looked at leaders and said to myself with more than my share of arrogance, "I can do it better." And yet I kept choosing to sit on the sidelines and criticize them from afar while they chose to put themselves in harm's way. The moment my own leadership potential began to unfold was when I stopped worrying about how others were leading and focused on my own effectiveness. Harm's way for me was starting my own consulting firm.

It began when I awoke from a dream in the middle of the night, acutely aware that for my life to feel complete, I had to strike out on my own as a consultant. I admitted to myself that I had too often compromised those desires in the interest of making "safe" money, and my heart and soul had suffered. After a long night of soul searching, I decided to compromise no more.

That morning I told my wife about the dream and my reflections on my life and career. I told her that I now knew, as powerfully as I had ever known anything, that it was time to start my own firm. To make this dream come true, I said, I needed to risk everything, including my relationship with her. I told her that I didn't want to lose her but that I needed to know if she was willing to accept this peril for the sake of my deepest desire. To this day her response brings tears to my eyes; I remember it as if it were yesterday. "Keith, I would be lying to you if I said that I did not want the life we have. I enjoy our house, our fine cars, and the lifestyle we lead. But these are not what I'm about. They are simply a preference. Go for your dream and know that I am with you all the way, no matter what losses we may face."

I opened my little consulting firm the following week and got my first client. Two weeks later I got another. Within a few months I was earning a comfortable living and have never looked back. Now I have partners who share my dream and a growing, thriving firm.

Too often in this world we stand back and criticize, as I had done much of my life. We sit on the sidelines rendering judgment on those who dare to make the tough decisions. But at least those leaders are taking their best shot, willing to risk the criticism and the consequences. And while I may not agree with the decisions they make, I admire them for their commitment to take a stand. This commitment is the secret ingredient.

We often think it's courage that distinguishes great leaders from others, and perhaps that is true, but behind that I see a commitment to be a player in the game. Larry Flick risked his life savings to build a company that redefined home services. Author-entrepreneur Joseph Jaworski threw away a promising career to start a new line of work, with nothing to go on but a belief in himself and a desire to make a difference. Kartar Singh has persevered for thirty years to achieve his dream of world peace. Their willingness to think big emboldens us all to believe that we can do the same, no matter how large or small the step may be.

> *I admire them for their commitment to take a stand. This commitment is the secret ingredient.*

Walter Wintle captured this spirit in his poem *Think Big* when he said, "Life's battles don't always go to the strongest or fastest...but sooner or later, the person who wins is the person who thinks he can." At the end of the day, it's that special moment when you choose to step into the void and say, "It is up to me," that makes all the difference. Such moments can come at any time, and when they do, the potential to become a remarkable leader is revealed in us all.

✧

We have now come full circle in our journey and arrived at the place from which we began. Perhaps it is too trite to say that great leadership starts and ends with yourself, but it does. In *The Wizard of Oz*, the wizard pointed out to Dorothy that she had the ability to go home all along, and in much the same spirit, we all have the ability to become a remarkable leader. It has nothing to do with luck, circumstance, good breeding, or any other factors that so many of us tend to turn to for solace. It has all to do with claiming your self—your deepest capacity to live life fully and authentically. And if taking a big swing is the secret ingredient, here is the full recipe:

✧ **Get clear about who you are and what you believe in;**

✧ **Follow your own muse;**

✧ **Accept and love yourself fully;**

✧ **Step up to the plate and take a big swing.**

In many ways we've all known these all along but wished it were more complex to give us an excuse for never playing full out. And some of us wanted *easier* steps that didn't require such an inward journey. I never met an extraordinary leader, though, who entertained such notions. They simply locked onto their commitment and never looked back.

KEY POINTS IN CHAPTER 12

- Great leadership and personal responsibility go hand in hand.

- Great leaders believe in themselves.

- To become a great leader one must stand for something significant. To be a great leader, take a big swing.

EPILOGUE

$\diamond$

HOW DO WE KNOW WHAT WE KNOW?

There are roughly three schools of thought regarding how one comes to *know* a particular truth about human nature: the scientific approach, careful observation, and inner knowing. In the scientific approach, it is believed that understanding anything requires one to break things down into their constituent parts, isolate key variables, and test the relationship between these variables using objective measures. The social sciences have struggled to become legitimate in the eyes of the scientific community by applying this model to a highly subjective and mysterious set of dynamics—human beings and their beliefs and behaviors. While progress has been made in certain areas of this investigation, I question the validity of such an approach in the arena of leadership, which is beset by a complex body of conflicting results—as illustrated at the beginning of this book.

The observational approach, adopted by phenomenologists, ethnomethodologists, anthropologists, and others, tells us that the best way to understand human beings is simply to observe their "natural" behaviors and then describe them, without explanation or evaluation. Unfortunately, being human themselves, those researchers can never completely disengage from their own biases and subjectivity, and so their attempts at objectivity are inevitably compromised—at best they can make good guesses. This is especially true in trying to unravel the cause-and-effect dynamics of leadership. There are no absolutes; how a leader responds to one situation might change in another and change again when faced with that same original situation.

The "inner-knowing" school of thought says that deep down, when we calm ourselves enough to sense and feel the truth, we will see clearly what is going on in front of us. But alas, our ego, our biases, and our conditioning make it very difficult to access that level. Even when we think we're in touch with our inner wisdom and guidance, we can be fooled, and no one is immune.

So how do I know that what I'm offering here is true and has value? I don't! To claim my research reflects some ultimate objectivity would be folly, for it has my own values written all over it. Rather than view it as research, then, I offer my efforts as an exploration, a journey of sorts, into discovering what is true for me and maybe true for others. My intent is to open up a dialogue and encourage a deeper search, for I am not satisfied with the conclusions being presented in the current literature of leadership under the guise of "scientific truth." This belief is shared by management professor Phil Rosenzweig, who wrote the paradigm-rattling book *The Halo Effect . . . and the Eight Other Business Delusions That Deceive Managers.*[1] It challenged the research and assumptions underlying many popular business ideas and theories. Inspired by the deeper inquiry that this book represents, I've been interested not in what has been observed of traditional leadership but in what kind of leadership *moves* me—inspires me to reach beyond myself and take meaningful and even life-changing actions. And in this inquiry, the answer of what moves me may be different than what moves you, making the exploration that much richer, for there is no universal template.

Nevertheless, when I shut my eyes, listened with an open heart, and stripped away as much of my expectations as I could, I began to see that remarkable leadership has something to do with an inner solidity that naturally shows up as ease, openness, and powerful determination. One gifted with a golden flame manifests a powerful presence that all of us can sense. In the recent U.S. Presidential election, for example, no matter your politics or beliefs, it was hard not to notice how Barack Obama carried himself—with considerable dignity and maturity, and how he has conducted himself since attaining the presidency. Here is a man clearly solid in himself and following his inner compass. And in my estimation, this leaves that crucial role of U.S. President in good steady hands.

Throughout my quest, I was reminded time and time again of Henry David Thoreau's famous saying: *If a man does not keep pace with his companions, perhaps it is because he hears a different drummer. Let him step to the music which he hears, however measured or far away.* This is the stuff of great leadership and what I saw, felt, experienced, and ultimately embraced in those who shared their stories with me.

In the end, though, even that discovery wasn't the final pot of gold in my quest to unlock the keys to remarkable leadership. Something else occurred that made my exploration the journey of a lifetime—I discovered what was true for *me*. My search for great leaders wasn't about finding new heroes or consoling myself that such people existed but about finding my own inner tiller and owning the leader in me.

> *I began to see that remarkable leadership has something to do with an inner solidity that naturally shows up as ease, openness, and powerful determination.*

This is ultimately the journey that all great leaders—and anyone who seeks to live a deeply satisfying life—eventually take: finding what is true for them. Yes, remarkable leaders are not much different than you and me; they are still human beings, with failings and weaknesses like us all. Indeed, they would likely be the first to admit that. They simply decided to follow their inner guidance and express their truths, trusting that while the choices they were making and the path they chose might not be perfect, at least they were their own.

Only when we boldly embrace our own unique path will we come to fully accept, appreciate, and respect that others might genuinely take a different path. To the extent that my path, my values, and my inner guidance system resonate with yours, then perhaps we can meet and join our efforts in something extraordinary; and if they do not, then let's honor the magnificent differences. When human beings mature enough to celebrate those differences, leaving room for other paths that are life-giving and life-sustaining, we will truly live together in peace on this planet.

Acknowledgements

Few non-fiction books are written alone and this one is no exception. While the ideas and their expression are mine, they have been influenced and improved by many others who have participated in some way. I am first and foremost deeply grateful to Matthew Gilbert, whose wise guidance and careful editing has helped shape the book and make the words far better crafted that I could have done alone. A huge thank you goes to the people who reviewed early copies of the book and offered both kind encouragement as well as extremely useful feedback. They include Ric Rudman, Timothy Swords, Jeannie Fay-Snow, Paul Downs, and Steve Tennant. Many people's ideas and conversations with me have helped me clarify my own thoughts on the subject of leadership. They include Bill Torbert, David Bradford, Ron Tilden, my dearly departed business partner Mike McKeon, to name a few. I am grateful to all my business partners, whose loving encouragement has and continues to fuel my efforts. They include Martha Borst, Marty Kaplan, Bill Stevens, the aforementioned Steve Tennant, Mark Voorsanger, and Annelisa MacBean.

And most importantly, I am deeply indebted to the 36 great leaders who have given me so much of their time and even more importantly, their inspiration. It is from their words and more importantly deeds that have taught me so much about leadership and I hope, through this book, will teach others. In alphabetical order, they are:

Peter Baretto, TORLYS
Betsy Bernard, AT&T
Robert Bobb, City Manager of D.C.
Dennis Boyle, IDEO
Paul Centenari, Acme Container Corp
Chris Chavez, Advanced Neuromodulation Systems
Suzanne Dibianca, Salesforce.com Foundation
Peter Farrell, ResMed

Larry Flick, Prudential, Fox and Roach

Jennifer Floren, Experience.com

Charles Garcia, Sterling Financial Investment

Ginger Graham, Amylin

Helen Greiner, I-Robot

Gordon Gund, Gund Enterprises

Bannus Hudson, BevMo

Jerry Jampolsky, Center for Attitudinal Healing,
    recently renamed Corstone

Joseph Jaworski, Generon Consulting

Scott Johnson, Myelin Repair Foundation

Guy Jordan, CR Bard

Kevin Kennedy, JDS Uniphase

Chuck Ledsinger, Choice Hotels

Atef Mankarios, Mankarios Partners

Larry Marton, Cellgate

Randy Meier, Advanced Medical Optics

Steve Newberry, LAM Research

Mihir Parikh, Aquest Systems

Judith Rogala, Flagship Express, Fed Ex

Will Rosenzweig, Republic of Tea

Mimi Silbert, Delancey Street Foundation

Kartar Singh, Golden Temple

Chauncey Starr, EPRI

Karen Talmadge, Kyphon

Mary Taverna, Hospice by the Bay

James Thrall, Chairman of Radiology, Massachusetts General Hospital

David White, New York Dance Theater Workshop

Andrea Youngdahl, Human Services, City of Oakland

Resources

For those of you who want to learn more about our efforts to cultivate remarkable leadership, we have built a website devoted to this aim. The website is www.remarkableleaders.com and will be launched as of 12/15/2009. There you will find my blog where I riff on the subject of leadership and offer observations as I walk about my life, resources that will be intriguing, information about my speaking to audiences on the subject of The Golden Flame, other books worth reading, etc. Please feel free to sign up and become a member.

For those of you who would like to be a closer friend of the remarkable leadership effort, you can by participating in a vibrant and growing community of leaders, all committed to deepening their leadership effectiveness over time. The most valuable part of that community is the leadership learning groups that I personally facilitate. Members of the learning groups consistently experience significant breakthroughs in their leadership ability and behavior. This is its goal and what we are all committed to accomplish for others and ourselves. Members of the groups also share resources, ideas, and lessons learned freely with one another in a safe and reinforcing setting. These groups have already begun. If you want more information about the groups, see the remarkable leaders website. If interested in joining a group, please contact me at kmerron3@comcast.net.

Notes

CHAPTER 1: THE PROBLEM OF LEADERSHIP
[1] Davis, J. A., T.W. Smith, and P.V Marsden, General Social Survey 1972-2004 Cumulative Code Book, University of Chicago, National Opinion Research Center, 2005.
[2] 2007 National Leadership Index, published by the Center for Public Leadership, John F. Kennedy School of Government, Harvard University.
[3] Howard, A. and R. Wellins, Global Leadership Forecast 2008/2009, a Development Dimensions International Bi-annual Survey Report.
[4] Kouzes, J. and B. Posner, The Leadership Challenge, New York: John Wiley & Sons, 2000.
[5] Goleman, D., "Leadership That Gets Results," Harvard Business Review, March-April 2000.
[6] See for example, Ryan, A., M. Schmit, and R. Johnson, "Attitudes and Effectiveness: Examining at an Organizational Level", Personnel Psychology, Winter 1996, pp. 853-882; and, Ostroff, C., "The Relationship Between Satisfaction, Attitudes & Performance: An Organizational Level Analysis," Journal of Applied Psychology, December 1992, pp. 963-974; and Griffeth, R., P. Hom, and S. Gaertner, "A Meta-Analysis of Antecedents and Correlates of Employee Turnover," Journal of Management, vol. 26, number 3, 2000, p. 479.
[7] Zenger, J. and J. Folkman, The Extraordinary Leader: Turning Good Managers into Great Leaders, New York: McGraw-Hill, 2002.
[8] Driving Business Results Through Continuous Engagement 2008/2009, a Watson-Wyatt WorkUSA Survey Report.

CHAPTER 2: THE ESSENCE OF REMARKABLE LEADERSHIP
[1] Harvey, A., Teachings of Rumi, Boston: Shambhala Books, 1999, p. 72.
[2] I conducted a careful content analysis by transcribing all of the interviews, going through them paragraph by paragraph and sentence by sentence, and then identifying common themes. In some cases, the themes were self-evident as they spoke directly to the importance of care, humility, honesty, etc. In others the themes had to be inferred from the stories they told. I am deeply grateful to Pam Williams, my research aide in this process.
[3] There are many examples. One in particular, based on thorough research, is the list developed by Zenger and Folkman in their book, The Extraordinary Leader. They listed the following as key attributes of outstanding leaders: high integrity, technical and professional expertise, solving problems and analyzing issues, innovation, practicing self-development, focus on results, establish stretch goals, take responsibility for outcomes, communicating powerfully and prolifically, inspiring and motivating others to high performance, building relationships, developing others, collaboration and teamwork, developing strategic perspectives, championing change, and connecting internal groups with the outside world. See Zenger, J. and J. Folkman, The Extraordinary Leader: Turning Good Managers into Great Leaders, New York: McGraw-Hill, 2002, pp. 103-108.
[4] Seneca, Letters from a Stoic, Penguin Classics, 1969, translated by Robin Campbell.

CHAPTER 3: THE COMPASS OF PURPOSE

[1] Longfellow, H., *A Psalm of Life*, Unknown Binding, 1855.

[2] Meade M., *The World Behind the World*, Greenfire Press, 2008.

[3] As described in Wikipedia, 2008, *A Course in Miracles* (also referred to as ACIM or The Course), written by Dr. Helen Schucman and Dr. William Thetford, describes a new approach to spirituality based on Christian teachings. Schucman dictated the book as delivered by an inner voice, which she described as coming from a divine source—Jesus Christ. The book uses traditional Judeo-Christian terminology but is not aligned to the doctrines of any one religion, denomination, or spiritual tradition. See Schucman, H. and W. Thetford, *A Course in Miracles*, Mill Valley: Foundation for Inner Peace, 1976.

[4] Hillman, J., *The Soul's Code: In Search of Character and Calling*, New York: Warner Books, 1996.

[5] See, for example, McClelland, D.C. and D. H. Burnham, "Power is the Great Motivator," *Harvard Business Review*, vol. 54, 1976, pp. 100-111.

CHAPTER 4: A CLEAR MAP

[1] There are far too many studies to report here. For reference material, see Lawler, E. *Employee Involvement and Total Quality Management*; U.S. Department of Labor report in 1993, *High Performance Work Practices and Firm Performance*; Bass, B., *Stogdill's Handbook of Leadership*, New York: The Free Press, 1976; Levin, D. and L. Tyson, *Participation, Productivity, and the Firm's Environment, in Paying for Productivity*, edited by Alan Blinder, Unknown Binding, 1989.

[2] Delivered on October 24, 2002 at the 9th Annual Business Women's Network Women & Diversity Leadership Summit, Washington, D.C.

[3] Hess, Edward D., *The Road to Organic Growth: How Great Companies Consistently Grow Market Share From Within*, New York: McGraw-Hill, 2007.

CHAPTER 5: THE ANCHOR OF VALUES

[1] George, B., *True North: Discover Your Authentic Leadership*, San Francisco: Jossey-Bass, 2007.

[2] Borrowed from Boulay, A., *Malden Hills: A Study in Leadership*, Quality Monitor Newsletter, October, 1996.

[3] Carlzon, J., *Moments of Truth*, Cambridge: Ballinger Publishing Company, 1987.

[4] Adapted from Samuel M. Janney, *The Life of William Penn; With Selections from His Correspondence and Auto-Biography*. Philadelphia: Hogan, Perkins, and Co., 1852. (Chapter 3, pp. 42-43; from the copy in Spruance Library, Bucks County Historical Society.)

CHAPTER 6: CARING AS A PASSION

[1] Campbell, J., *Pathways to Bliss*, Novato: New World Library, 2004.

[2] Greene, L. and J. Sharman-Burke, *The Mythic Journey: The Meaning of Myth as a guide for Life*, Canada: Fireside, 2000, p. 211.

[3] Ibid., p. 217.

[4] Borrowed from www.barefootsworld.net.

CHAPTER 7: A ROCK-SOLID SENSE OF SELF
[1] See http://www.kaiserfamilyfoundation.org/rxdrugs/market.cfm for more information.
[2] For an early historical reference of Gurdjieff's teaching, see Ouspensky, P. D., *In Search of the Miraculous,* Florida: Harcourt, Inc., 1949.
[3] Jung, C. G., "Analytical Psychology and Weltanshauung," *The Structure and Dynamics of the Psyche,* Princeton University Press, 1989, p. 737.

CHAPTER 8: THE POWER OF SELF-COMPASSION
[1] Maslow, A. H., *The Psychology of Science,* Chicago: Henry Regnery Company, 1969.

CHAPTER 9: LEADERSHIP AND THE SOUL
[1] In the late '60s, Ralph Stogdill underwent a systematic review and analysis of the literature on leadership and produced a voluminous book in 1974. The literature was vast, and yet there was no agreement about what leadership is, or what good leadership is all about. Stogdill's handbook on leadership, revised and last published in 1981, described well over 1000 studies on leadership and was almost as thick as the Bible. Again, no conclusion. To make the point rather blunt, there are over 6000 books currently listed on Amazon.com on the subject of leadership. And in spite of this, we still don't have a shared understanding of the deeper qualities and characteristics that constitute great leadership.
[2] Bennis, W., and B. Nanus, *Leaders: Strategies for Taking Charge,* New York: Harper Collins, 1985.
[3] Borrowed and slightly reworded from Hay, P., *The Book of Business Anecdotes,* New York: Facts on File, 1988, p. 178.
[4] Deal, T., and A. Kennedy, *Corporate Cultures,* New York: Perseus Books Publishers, L.L.C., 1982.
[5] Moss Kanter, R., *Change Masters,* New York: Simon & Schuster, Inc., 1983.
[6] A notable exception to this is the book, Managing for Excellence, co-written with Allen Cohen by my good friend, David Bradford. The book did an excellent job of raising questions about heroic leadership and its limitations. See: Cohen, A. and D. Bradford, *Managing for Excellence,* New York: John Wiley & Sons, Inc., 1984.
[7] Hillman, J., *The Soul's Code: In Search of Character and Calling,* New York: Warner Books, 1996.
[8] Interview with Bill Plotkin shown on the Animus Valley Institute website in 2007.
[9] Pfeiffer, J., "The Men's Wearhouse: Success in a Declining Industry," Case HR-5, Stanford, CA: Graduate School of Business, Stanford University, 1997, p. 4.
[10] Meade, M., *The World Behind the World,* Seattle: Greenfire Press, 2008, p. 9.
[11] Barker, J., *Future Edge,* New York: Harper Collins, 1992.
[12] "Peter Drucker." Quotes.net. STANDS4 LLC, 2009. 3 July. 2009. http://www.quotes.net/quote/6632
[13] Greenhouse, Steven, "How Costco Became the Anti-Wal-Mart," *NY Times,* July 17, 2005.

CHAPTER 10: THE EVOLUTION OF LEADERSHIP

[1] This section was drawn heavily from my doctoral dissertation: *The Relationship Between Ego Development and Managerial Effectiveness Under Conditions of Uncertainty,* Cambridge, MA: Harvard Graduate School of Education, 1985.

[2] Loevinger, J., "Construct Validity of the Sentence Completion Test of Ego Development," *Applied Psychological Measurement,* vol. 3, 1979, pp. 281-311.

[3] Harvey, O.J., D.E. Hunt, and H.M. Schroder, *Conceptual Systems and Personality Organization,* New York: John Wiley and Sons, 1961.

[4] McCrae, R. and P. Costa, "Openness to Experience and Ego Level in Loevinger's Sentence Completion Test: Dispositional Contributions to Developmental Models of Personality," *Journal of Personality and Social Psychology,* vol. 39, no. 6, 1980, pp. 1179-1190.

[5] Bartunek, J., J. Gordon, and R. Weathersby, "Developing 'Complicated' Understanding in Administration," *Academy of Management Review,* vol. 8, no. 2, 1983, pp. 273-84.

[6] Joiner, W., and S. Josephs, *Leadership Agility,* San Francisco: Jossey-Bass, 2007.

[7] Cook-Greuter, S. *Post-autonomous ego development: A study of its nature and measurement,* Doctoral dissertation, Cambridge, MA: Harvard Graduate School of Education, 1999. For more information, see also Torbert, W.R., *Managing the Corporate Dream,* Homewood: Dow Jones-Irwin, 1987.

[8] Kegan, R., *The Evolving Self: Problem and Process in Human Development,* Cambridge: Harvard University Press, 1982.

[9] Piaget, J., *The Moral Judgment of the Child,* Glencoe: The Free Press, 1948.

CHAPTER 11: BECOMING A REMARKABLE LEADER

[1] Campbell, J., *The Hero With a Thousand Faces,* New York: Princeton University Press, 1949, pp. 19-20.

[2] Campbell, J., Ibid, p. 30.

[3] I am deeply grateful to my good friend and colleague Grady McGonagill who developed this particular model. It is at the core of a training program he has created that helps leaders learn how to find and strengthen their own natural leadership style.

CHAPTER 12: THE SECRET INGREDIENT

[1] This passage is often incorrectly attributed to Nelson Mandela's 1994 Inaugural Address. Williamson in her website offers an explanation: *"Several years ago, this paragraph from A RETURN TO LOVE began popping up everywhere, attributed to Nelson Mandela's 1994 Inaugural Address. As honored as I would be had President Mandela quoted my words, indeed he did not. I have no idea where that story came from, but I am gratified that the paragraph has come to mean so much to so many people."*

EPILOGUE: HOW DO WE KNOW WHAT WE KNOW?

[1] Rosenzweig, P., *The Halo Effect...and Eight Other Business Delusions That Deceive Managers,* New York: Free Press, 2007.